DO THE RIGHT THING

in Business Improvement, Including Process and Technology

DAVID A. DURYEA

WESTBOW
PRESS®
A DIVISION OF THOMAS NELSON
& ZONDERVAN

WestBow Press books may be ordered through booksellers or by contacting:

WestBow Press
A Division of Thomas Nelson & Zondervan
1663 Liberty Drive
Bloomington, IN 47403
www.westbowpress.com
1 (866) 928-1240

ISBN: 978-1-4908-8606-0 (sc)
ISBN: 978-1-4908-8607-7 (hc)
ISBN: 978-1-4908-8605-3 (e)

Library of Congress Control Number: 2015910172

Print information available on the last page.

WestBow Press rev. date: 11/2/2016

CONTENTS

DEDICATION

To Laura — my friend, wife and love. Thanks for encouraging me to get the book done.

ACKNOWLEDGEMENTS

No book can be written without help from many people such as the team of publishing professionals at Westbow Press. My thanks to you all for your support and partnership.

In addition to the many people from whom I have learned over the course of my career, a special word of thanks is due to a few key people.

Thank you to Dr. SJA Williams for his undying support, for his insistence on clarity, and for testing my thinking to ensure the concepts were sound.

Thank you to Bill Blankschaen, writer and content strategist, for editing, creative input, and helping me understand the publishing industry.

Thanks also to Harold Smith, a friend and fellow book lover who encouraged me to continue to develop this project.

And finally, special thanks to my entire family for patiently sharing my time and understanding all the work required to publish a book.

PREFACE

This book puts into plain words the way you can embrace, understand, and attain reality-based business improvement. It clearly explains the reason a business exists, profitable operation, process-based performance, and technology enablement. It is a holistic approach that starts with the core of a business and drives all the way through successful improvement initiatives that gain true value.

This book is based on my observation of facts, not unproven strategies or suppositions. As a legal expert witness, forensics and innovation specialist for over thirty-two years (including over sixty improvement projects), I found this method to be solid, foundational, and needed for reality-based improvement. The book covers misguided leadership styles, failed enablement initiatives, and disintegrated operation models that have led not only to the destruction of an organization's projects but also to their utter demise. In turn, use these methods correctly and you could drive your company to be an industry best-in-class leader.

These principles are strategic yet pragmatic. These practices will help a company defy the next economic downturn, incubate a new venture, or reinvent your organization to the next level of performance. If you are in any way involved in your company's business improvement as a business professional, technology manager, or engaged executive leader, you will find these principles successful, reality based, and ultimately the right thing for your company.

FOUNDATIONAL PRINCIPLE

An organization is of God. It has been created to emulate God because he made it. You can see him in it and through it. It is the very essence and likeness. That is why it works.

INTRODUCTION

Recently, a colleague of mine named John (which is his middle name) came to me with a dilemma. He is an innovation and technology leader in a company faced with an improvement project that uses a mix of technology, business process, and organizational change across multiple business lines. Each function had different lines of authority, leaders, and agendas. Most of these leaders did not want the proposed changes. These alleged improvements would change their functional operation and make them modify their own departments. In fact, he explained the other leaders actually tried to stop him through passive-aggressive behavior, appearing to help while letting him fail.

He asked me this question: "What do I do when leaders do not want to see the duplicity of their operation? They simply cannot or will not look at our organization and see how they are inhibiting performance by their siloed view, protectionism, and self-preservation. Coupled with our organization's dismal technology-implementation track record, I do not know what to do."

Unfortunately, this situation is typical in many organizations where personnel who are tasked with business improvement are resisted by internal politics, self-preservation, and poor internal project performance. It takes a lot of energy and self-determination to bring about change in an organization. Sometimes, it takes a paradigm shift in culture, thinking, and approaches because economics, industry forces, or internal pressures prevent real improvement. A group, team, or just an individual can put a company on the right track if that group or individual knows how to navigate reality-based business improvement.

I know John understands that business improvement takes into account many factors that sometimes are not optimal for the individual business leader, especially if the organizational leaders do not have a holistic point of view. I asked him, "Have you considered the costs and benefits of each of solution?" He replied, "Yes, and it would bring about the best performance for the company. I know it is best for the organization." John looked at me with a look that I have seen much too often from professionals that have sincere motives to make their organization excel, yet it prevents optimal performance. I looked back and with an encouraging voice and said, "Well then, if you have done everything the best way you know, then you know what you must do. So just do the right thing."

Instinctively, John knew what to do; he just needed someone to encourage him that what he was proposing was the *right* thing to do. Unlike John, many businesspeople, including the leadership, cannot articulate the best solutions for their organization and resist new ideas and innovations. Leadership is often ignorant, afraid, or unwilling to see what makes real impact. They consider parts of an organization but fail to see the entire enterprise when a significant project is undertaken. In fact, many technology and improvement projects are half-dead before they even start because they did not consider true business-improvement concepts. This is a staggering realization and must be turned around for your organization to maintain viability.

You see, many organizations do not realize they are dying. Without any improvement or intervention, either the next economic or industry shift will see their business forced into dissolution. This is why we need to improve the business the right way so that your organization will be healthy and viable, able to withstand market shifts and economic downturns, and continue to serve your customers in the best way possible.

To improve the business the right way, you must first understand the components of a business not from a single-minded book, thought, or idea but from the customer's point of view, because in the end, the customer is the one paying for the product or service. We also need to study how a business really works and the components that make a viable operation that is profitable and healthy. We also need to understand real business performance not just from a myopic point of reference or a set of misguided analytics but also from organizational goals the way the original vision was intended.

We will be exploring major parts of business improvement including an organization's operations, process, technology, and exactly how to recognize the correct type of improvement for an organization. These include not just methods, methodologies, standards, or templates but also the essence of the business itself and the reason why projects underperform or fail completely. All of this is exciting, perplexing, and required so we can improve the business the right way.

In some cases, these ideas will be a major change in the status quo and even earthshaking for existing technology, process, and improvement leadership. It will require steadfastness, mental toughness, perseverance, and committed resolve. But in the end, you will perform for the company as a whole and be able to say, "Yes, I did the right thing for the company."

The first part of the journey is to understand the common thread throughout all improvement failures. We need to understand what reality-based business strategy looks like and to understand what really matters to an organization that drives performance. Before embarking on any improvement project, one must understand what is at the core of improvement and the strategy to embrace it. Let's begin the journey into reality-based business improvement.

PART 1

BUSINESS BASICS: BUSINESS STRATEGY STRUCTURE

CHAPTER 1

BUSINESS AND THE COMMON THREAD

It is hard to define business improvement without first defining business. A business is an organization that focuses on achieving a goal. The goal is what defines a business and is the center of how an organization is built. Before one can achieve business improvement, one must know the goal of the organization and the rules of operation to achieve that goal. If there is no goal, then there is no reason to organize. This might sound obvious; one cannot have an operation that achieves nothing or doesn't have a target, goal, or mission. Failure would be inevitable. A business must have a goal to organize and to operate. No goal. No organization. No business.

Also, a *perceived* goal can be worse than no goal. A perceived goal is one that is believed to be reality but is not. If an operation has been built around a perceived goal, the organization will expend resources to achieve a goal that is based in someone's fantasy or an idea of reality. This will waste resources, capital, and time. Wasting resources is the worst offense of any improvement professional. We have limited resources when embarking on any project. Losing skills, capital, and other assets that could be used to further a company's potential is counter to business improvement.

A similar offense is heading a misguided project that could lead a company into dissolution or bankruptcy. One thing is guaranteed: if you are continually focused on a perceived goal, the organization you serve will wastefully consume resources and eventually fail. The reality of outside forces, customer needs, and competition will erode a company to the point of insolvency. A perceived goal that is not based on the organization's main goal is worse than not having a goal at all. At least in not having a goal, a company would either prevent wasting resources or not begin a startup process. One must understand and know the real goal to organize, use resources correctly, and achieve success.

As defined here, a business is organized to achieve a known and real goal. We will cover the understanding of that goal, business strategy, and the composition for company success. We will also cover the basis for project success and failures and the effect on overall organization success. Let's begin by understanding the common thread through many organizations: the centric and basic operational goal.

The Common Thread

Organizations are always on the move. They are either expanding or contracting. They react to environments in which they operate, including changes in governments, resources, culture, and markets. They constantly need change and improvement in order to continue a profitable operation. Without successful business-improvement initiatives, a company's continued performance will be in jeopardy.

But business-improvement success or failure is squarely on an organization's leadership ability to manage an initiative to improve the enterprise. This sounds pretty basic and obvious, but the interesting revelation is that many COOs, CFOs, CIOs, and even CEOs do not know how to interpret the true value of an improvement initiative for their organization. This is hard to swallow, but just look at the data surrounding the success (failure) rates of improvement and technology innovation projects.

- o 83 percent project failure rate and budget overruns in 1994 (The Standish Group 1994)
- o 72 percent project failure rate and budget overruns in 2000 (The Standish Group 2010)

- ○ 71 percent project failure rate and budget overruns in 2004 (The Standish Group 2010)
- ○ 68 percent project failure rate and budget overruns in 2008 (The Standish Group 2010)
- ○ 70 percent project failure rate and budget overruns current (Cantara, et al. 2014)
- ○ $209 billion lost on failed projects in 1994 (The Standish Group 1994)
- ○ $3.7 trillion spent on IT (Gartner 2013)

I believe anyone who has been in the technology or business-improvement industry for at least ten years has seen the effects of these dismal statistics or struggled with his or her own failing improvement project. With trillions of dollars spent on projects[1] that struggle or are canceled completely, leaders have to deal with these facts. Many of these leaders have fallen victims to endless organizational restructures or from project fallouts claiming improved performance with these new projects. As you can see from the statistics above, the rate of project failures or underperformance continues to be above 68 percent. It sounds like the industry of business and technology improvement is not improving business at all, especially if you factor the costs of all projects that have failed. It is a very expensive endeavor to spend resources on projects that fail most of the time.

So what is the cause of these failures?

In overseeing, reviewing, or participating in upward of sixty business- and technology-improvement projects from all aspects, including strategizing, implementing, and failed project reviews through expert witness forensics, I have seen a basic element that was common in each failure. It was not the single aspect of project management, project resources, executive sponsorship, or even requirement's definition. A common thread was that leadership did not implement a project that empowered the organization's most basic goal. The most basic goal is the organization's core business model.

To have success, management must relate every improvement initiative to an organization's core business model. The core business

---

[1]

model is central to organizational improvement from all aspects, including process, technology, and any innovation enablement.

During the course of this book, we will connect the core business model of an organization to improvement performance. To understand the core business model, we must first understand the law of business reality. So let's explore the foundation of business improvement. The common thread through all organization starts with the exploration of the law of business reality.

CHAPTER 2

THE LAW OF BUSINESS REALITY

The law of business reality is real. Its aspect is real, its affects are real, and in the end, the results are real. It is the basis for all successful organizations. It is an understanding in practice rather than stated perceptions. The basic elements are understood by experiences rather than logical reasoning or operational concepts. You cannot escape it, and if you ignore the law, it will eventually bring reality to your organization.

Business reality is that an organization exists to serve its customers in a profitable way. The law is if either factor changes, not serving customers or unprofitable performance, the company will cease to exist.

> **The Law of Business Reality**—Organizations serve customers in a profitable way or cease to exist.

It seems simple and obvious, but it is a fact. It is the reality of business. But many leaders act as though they do not believe this law. They state it in their minds, but their actions do not reflect that they fully believe it. You can see it as they make decisions on a daily basis. Let's explore the two parts of the law to gain further insight into why leaders miss this important aspect of reality.

The first part of the law—serving your customer—is paramount. Organizations that do not serve their customers will lose focus and start to perform or operate in a way that is serving their own organizations, government influences, or some other area that is vying for their resources. An organization that loses focus on customer needs, trends, and future needs will open an opportunity for other companies to capitalize on the void. That is what happens. A customer wants his needs to be fulfilled. If there are other companies that serve customers better, who have built a better "mousetrap," they will gain customers and grab market share.

Losing customers is the quickest way to lose revenue. When you see the market share shift, there is a doubling effect. Every dollar that is shifted from your organization to another organization represents a negative dollar to you and a positive dollar to your competition. In reality, that is a two-dollar shift in the market position. It will not take long before you see the effects of lost market share. This can occur so quickly that it can—and has—brought down large companies in a single year.

Do you remember Arthur Andersen? Andersen, a company that had a history of serving its customers in the consulting and account industry since 1913, became the largest accountancy in the world (Wilson 2005). It lost its focus for one customer, Enron, and it sent their company's reputation on a downward spiral. It lost customer after customer until it basically ceased to exist as a viable company, and the rest was sold to competitors. Even though its criminal verdict was overturned by the United States Supreme Court, Arthur Andersen did not return as a viable business status *(The Chicago Tribune* 2012). It seemed to think it could operate above its customers' basic need—trust—and this sent the company into bankruptcy in just one year.

Another great example is General Motors. GM experienced great growth and enjoyed great customer loyalty, a trust, and a great brand that lasted into the 1960s. In the 1970s, GM shifted its focus to build cheaper cars and trucks because it had a hard time keeping up with demand *(Wikipedia* n.d.). When it made that shift, its product lost quality and opened the door for foreign manufacturers to build products with higher quality. Because of brand loyalty, which GM played up in advertising, it took some time to see the effects of not meeting customer needs. But in 2009, the unthinkable and unimaginable happened. GM filed for bankruptcy and was taken over by the federal government *(Ivy*

Business Journal 2009). Most of its competitors had a rough road but remained intact while GM was left to the courts.

In contrast, Toyota served customers and built a brand that kept it at the top of the automotive industry for multiple years. An envy of the automotive industry, Toyota built its foundation on the solid ground of serving the customer and reliability. When the storm came with the "sticking gas pedal" recall in the middle of the 2008–2009 recession, I remember Toyota was able to go back and pitch its history of reliability, which helped the company sustain its number one ranking through the storm (Cars.com n.d.).

A company must fulfill the basic need of a customer or the company will not be able to maintain a viable status. This is the first, most basic and paramount part of the law of business reality—serving the customer.

The second part of the law, operating in a profitable way, is also paramount. Let's describe "profitable way." Profit is generated from producing a product that is sold for less cost than it was produced. Two components are involved: the first is product/service quality and the second is efficient operation. Product/service quality goes hand in hand with meeting the needs of the customer. As stated with GM, it lost focus on meeting the need for product quality and lost market share.

Quality is based on the customer's definition of quality, not on the organization's. This is a big misunderstanding by many organizations. If a customer believes that a quality car should last at least 100,000 miles without any major breakdowns, then that is quality reality. If a customer believes that an investment firm should state the facts of an investment's full disclosure and loss, then that is quality reality. If a customer believes that milk should be drinkable at least three weeks after purchase (with normal refrigeration), then that is quality reality. Quality is based on the customer's belief and is totally measured by the customer. How well an organization meets its quality for a customer is the quality reality for the customer.

Efficiency simply means to develop a process that presents and delivers a product or service less costly than an organization can sell its goods or service. Once an organization sets out to meet the needs of customers, the organization needs to produce the product or service in an efficient manner. The efficiency process starts from the point of customer contact through product/service development, delivery, and servicing the product. It is the basic operation of any organization and is the most controllable for management. If you cannot develop a process that produces a product or service that is less cost than the price to sell it, then you cannot generate profit.

Efficiency is based on management's ability to manage. You must operate your company efficiently to generate a profit, or you will not last long in the marketplace. This seems simple, but it is amazing how so many leaders are so close to details that they cannot see where they are leaking profits. It is the essence of serving a customer; otherwise, a customer could go to a competitor or could perform or develop the product himself or herself. Think about it. When you consider a purchase, do you ask yourself, "Can I do this myself?" If you don't, then you should. A company's leadership should be able to control the efficient process management.

I found that the agricultural industry has a great handle on efficiency. Have you ever visited large farms or agricultural operations? They are amazing at how well they use and reuse almost every aspect/expense and reinvest into a profit-generating activity. One such operation is an egg farm that I was blessed to visit a few years back. It was so efficient that from sixteen million chickens, it produced eggs in a process that was so fully automated that, from the washing, grading, packing, and shipping, not a human hand was involved (except driving the trucks). Even the farms were so fully automated that the fans, lights, and feed were operated remotely. And of course, it used everything down to the chicken dung that was reprocessed and sold for fertilizer. Seems incredible, but it's very efficient. Like this agricultural company, management needs to understand that efficiency is paramount not just for success but for long-term sustainability.

Organizations need to fight to keep the balance among service, quality, and efficiency to continue its existence. The counterbalance of operation is meeting the needs of efficient production and the customer's expectation for quality. Each will pull in ways to either increase quality or product efficiency and is considered the greatest of all management dilemmas. The two, quality and efficiency, act as great counterbalance, which must be managed to meet goals for the customer and the organization. If you cannot produce a quality product or service, you will lose your customers to your competitors. Conversely, if you cannot produce a quality product efficiently, you will not generate profits. You will be out of balance and the company will lose customers and/or profits, which will lead to the organization's demise.

An example of this can be found in the construction industry. Building a house is all about designing to a customer's specific expectations and constructing with the lowest possible cost. In my experience, a building company's margins are between 8 percent and 12 percent for each construction project, with very little room to negotiate profit. When an alternation is made to a design, typically the builder will generate a "change order" and add costs to the total project. The art (balance) is to design enough base features into the base cost so that customers will accept all other change orders to the original design. I have seen upward of 30 percent and 40 percent increases from the base cost of a building project from change orders. The great balance is to make sure the builder does not cut what a customer would consider base items and move the direct costs to the purchaser. In other words, customer perceived "quality" is maintained within reasonable costs. It is the way the construction industry balances its thin margins and still hedges its profits.

The law of business reality is that an organization exists to serve customer's needs with quality and efficiency in a profitable way. Organizations need to balance the law with serving customers while providing quality and efficiency to produce a product or service that generates profitability. It is a difficult task, but it is the way an organization exists in the marketplace for today and is sustainable through the years.

You also cannot escape the law of business reality and the influences it has over your organization. If you do not believe this law, then I would stop and not continue to read the rest of the book. It will not make sense to you. That is how strong of a belief I have in understanding *reality* for your organization. But if you agree with the law and use it as a backdrop for understanding, you will have insights and success in all your business-improvement projects. Understand the law of business reality before the reality hits your organization.

Business-Improvement Model

Step 1 Understand the Law of Business Reality

Organizations serve customers in a profitable way (balance quality and efficiency) or cease to exist.

CHAPTER 3

CORE BUSINESS MODEL—ESSENCE OF AN ORGANIZATION

In any business-improvement engagement, whether it is process productivity, technology utilization, or full strategy review, one of the most important meetings is with the CEO, president, or owner. One such meeting was a very interesting one. I asked the owner of a large, privately owned RV manufacturer, "Why do people buy from your company as opposed to your competitors?" He pulled back from the desk and thought for a moment, and then he said, "That is a very interesting question that you asked me." Later, he stated, "You are the first consultant to ask me that question." What is interesting is that the owner instinctively knew the answer but others did not even know to ask a simple question about his organization.

That simple question actually leads to the reason why an organization exists in the first place. Meaning every company has a unique product or service that fulfills a need in the market. If a company did not meet a customer's needs, the company would not be in operation. Hence, every organization is a subset of the law business reality as the company profitably meets the needs of their customers. The way an organization meets the needs of its customers versus its competitors in a profitable way is called the *core business model* of the organization. To fully understand a core business model, let's first explore the meaning of two basic concepts: first, a business based on the law and second, a *common* business model.

Definition of a Business Based on the Law

What is a business? Previously, we described a business as an organization to achieve a goal. True, but with the definition of the law of business reality, we can further define a business. A business is an organization with a specific purpose that operates or transacts to deliver a product or service in exchange for some value. Whether the organization is a nonprofit, not-for-profit, or a for-profit structure, the organization is operating as a business. The basic test if a group is a business is to ask, "Does the organization receive some value for delivering or performing a service for a person or other organization?" If the answer is yes to that question, then your organization will transact as a business subject to the law of business reality.

Also, a business must be organized to operate. Sounds simplistic, but think about it. What is the first thing we think about when we are on a customer service phone call and we get the run around or do not get our answer? Plus, what if the product or service is not what we expect? We say, "That company is disorganized" or "They just do not get it." Instinctively, we know that a company should understand how to operate to meet our needs. But to do so, the company must have an inherited understanding of how to organize and operate to achieve its goals. That is why a business has inherited aspects of operation, inherited from meeting the law of business reality. Each business will transact and have basic operations to serve customers in a profitable way; otherwise, it will not be able to achieve its goal.

Definition of a Business Model

What is a business model? One of the best definitions is from an investor's or entrepreneur's point of reference. "A business model is a business concept or vision that meets customers' specific needs with a sustainable profit model." Sounds a bit like the law of business reality.

That is because a business model is derived from the law of business reality and is applied to a specific customer need that is fulfilled. If customers' specific needs can be met in a sustainable profitable operation, then the business model can be realized and is a sustainable concept. The key aspect is that the business concept is a workable and sustainable profit model for operation.

Why do investors look for a business model? An investor wants to invest in an organization that is viable for the short and long term. The investor looks for a sound business model and if the company understands how to sustain profit generation. If the model is sound, meaning that the profit generation from the business concept to execution can be attained, then an investor would consider investment in the company's ability to manage the business model execution. This is also known as operationalizing the business concept. The investor would then look for a business model that is managed efficiently. If so, the investor would then consider the company as a reasonable risk for investment. This also represents a business model that is operationally successful.

Core Business Model

The core business model is a type of business model. The core business model is simply an organization's unique business model to which it serves its customers and generates profit in its own industry versus its competitors. Another way to view the core business model is to ask why an organization makes profits in its industry differently from its competitors.

Think about it. If an organization cannot distinguish itself from other organizations, then it will have no unique identity, message, or worst of all, way to meet its customers' needs. In fact, the only thing that separates one organization from another is its unique way it meets their customers' needs. And if the organization cannot be profitable at meeting customers' needs, then the core business model in not operable.

Core Business Model—Serve customer uniquely in a profitable way, balancing quality and efficiency.

15

The core business model is more than just a business model. It is the *essence of why a company exists* and is the most significant and distinctive level of operation for an organization. It is the organization's ultimate goal. No company can operate without it, and no company will be viable without understanding it. Business-improvement successes or failures are based on management's ability to understand its influence and manage to their organization's core business model. I cannot overemphasize this point. Missing the core business model is missing the entire point of a business. I want to make sure that you understand this point by reviewing an example. The goal of the organization centers on the core business model of the organization. Let's compare three different companies in the same industry: pizza.

Consider three companies: Pizza Hut, Domino's Pizza, and Papa John's Pizza. They are all in the food service business and, more specifically, the pizza industry. They are all viable companies operating to meet their customers' needs and generate profits in different ways. Domino's is about speed. Remember the old *thirty minutes or it's free* slogan? Domino's Pizza, back then, never implied it had the best-tasting pizza but that it had reasonable taste and fast delivery. Since then, it has initiated a taste-improvement effort, but for the most part, it serves customers who do not want to wait for their food (Horovitz 2009). Its business model is based on developing and delivering pizza and other food items to its customers faster than its competitors. Domino's Pizza's core business model is fast, quality pizza (and other items) delivered to its customers.

Papa John's Pizza. What comes to mind is its slogan "Better ingredients. Better pizza" (PapaJohns.com n.d.). It has positioned itself as the best-tasting delivered pizza to its customers. Conversely, Papa John's never said it had the fastest pizza delivery but makes the case that it is the best-tasting delivered pizza. Its core business model is based on better ingredients to make a pizza yield a better-tasting delivered pizza. But it might take more than thirty minutes for delivery. Its customers are willing to wait more time for better-tasting pizza; hence, Papa John's Pizza's core business model is based on taste versus speed in pizza delivery.

Pizza Hut's original model is based on restaurant service. Pizza Hut does not claim fast delivery, but its model is based on having a restaurant experience while serving pizza as its main product. Pizza Hut does have a delivery service, but its base model has been the experience of great-tasting pizza in a traditional restaurant experience. Pizza Hut's core business model is based on the restaurant experience versus delivery.

All three companies—Domino's, Papa John's, and Pizza Hut—have different ways they serve their customers and have made sizable business profits based on their individual core business models. It is more than a marketing slogan or a concept for a campaign. The core business model is more than a concept or a philosophy; it is the reason a company exists and is the basis for all activity, service, and profitability.

Operation of the Core Business Model

How do core business models get their start? Well, that is a good question and one that needs to be understood. A core business model starts with a product or service idea, an idea to improve a consumer's situation. If one can improve the life of an individual or the operation of another organization, then meeting a consumer need is achieved. This is what is meant by stating "meeting the needs of a customer." If a product or service cannot meet the need of a customer and improve his or her situation, then there is no reason for the new product or service to be developed and introduced into the market.

Once a product or service has been established that meets the need of a customer, then what remains is the question "Can the product or service be developed marketed and transformed into a profitable operation?" This is where the introduction of the law of business reality is combined with the value of the product or service must produce a viable operation.

This transformation from product/service to a viable operation must be realized before a viable core business model is achieved. The transformation process begins with a product or service from its introduction state to its sustainable market state then to a profitable operation state. A product or service reaches a sustainable operation when the core business model becomes viable. This transformation is a difficult process and requires skilled management leadership, capital, and knowledge of the market. Otherwise, a great idea for a product or service can die before it even gets a chance in the market.

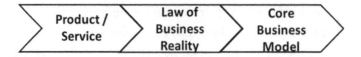

There are many different aspects of the transformation to a core business model to explore like product conversion, market identification, and operation realization. This is what makes a core business model so unique compared to other areas of society. The core business has a product, service, market, satisfying the customer, environment, and profitability all wrapped up in one. It is the product or service operational vision realized in a viable form. This is why a company has its most difficult operation in the first, third, and its fifth year of existence. This is true because these are the most critical years for moving from a service/product to a viable company. Let me explain.

The first year is when a product or service is in its most critical state of achieving success and when a customer will buy it for its base characteristics. In the first year, a customer may not buy the product or service for its base value.

In the third year is when the product or service has been accepted by a customer. The organization has been forming processes and operations to sustain a viable operation. But now the organization needs to duplicate and multiply for growth. If the company cannot achieve sustainable operations, the company will not be able to maintain viability.

The fifth year is when the organization has transformed from just a product want to a brand company. Where operations have performed, multiplied, and now they have built more sustainable products and services. This is also the time when capital and market may shift, and if the company does not have ample capital or market penetration, then an economic downturn could bring the company down quickly.

An example of this was found with a colleague of mine while I was with a financial institution. He was the owner of a successful IT consulting company. He had built the company up to a respectable size with IT development services and staff augmentation. When the great downturn in 2006 occurred, he saw his company that he built evaporate quickly. He told me, "One by one, I watched every one of my contracts canceled, and in the span of ninety days, my company was gone."

His company was a working, viable operation that had just started to gain momentum with capital. Once the contracts started to be canceled, his company could not move fast enough to regain viable operation. The company did not have adequate capital to maintain liquidity during a restructure of operations. His company went into bankruptcy. I knew many companies during that time that had the same fate. They were good companies that just did not have enough time to move out of the third area of viability—maintain capital for shifts in market changes or conditions.

Economics—Viability of a Core Business Model

There are lots of great ideas to which a potential company could be started. Many people have thoughts, ideas, and great vision for a company. The reality is the logistics to realize that vision many times do not make it economically feasible. A core business model is where the vision of operation and economics are plausible and sustainable for an organization. It is a fact that if you cannot make a profit consistently, then you cannot support a viable operation.

I have a colleague that comes up with some ideas for companies. The problem is he never seems to understand the economic side of the core business model. His latest was a mobile auto repair shop for gasoline automobiles. His plan was to have a portable lift that he could mount on an enclosed trailer to which he would drive up to a location and load a car to perform repairs. He would perform the repairs and then unload the car.

The issue is he did not consider environmental, zoning, and other governmental laws and the logistics of carrying all the tools required, performing the work, and properly disposing of fluids. When you take all that into consideration, plus the price point to which a customer will pay for the convenience of a mobile repair service, it did not make the endeavor economically feasible. Unless there were major changes in repair innovation and regulation, the idea of a mobile repair shop did not meet the core business model profitability litmus test or the base economics required to maintain a viable business model.

Think about the old example of a lemonade stand. Every summer on my street, children (including my own) set up a lemonade stand. It is great fun to see the neighborhood children have such entrepreneurial spirit. But if you think about it, the lemonade stand has its own economic core business model. As long as you can make lemonade that sells at a viable price point, let's say twenty-five cents per cup, they made a profit. The issue is that they only made profit when the outside temperature was eighty degrees or higher. So they had a very seasonal business and could only support operation for a few weeks a year. Yes, even a lemonade stand cannot escape the economic feasibility of a core business model and the law of business reality.

If an organization has been operating for any length of time, then the company has a viable core business model. The market and economic pressures will cause most businesses to collapse in one to five years if the core business model cannot support a profitable economic model. So if a company has any history of operation, then more than likely there is an active and sustainable core business model in operation.

Lessons From Two Tech Companies

To drive this point of the importance of the core business model let's review two companies that have completely missed its importance; uBeam and Yahoo. The criticality of understanding the customer and offering a solid product or service in a profitable way is paramount. For both uBeam and Yahoo, two companies that have suffered the fate of a failed venture because of missing this critical issue of the core business model. Let's review and find how these companies never seemed to find their core business model.

uBeam

uBeam once was the darling of the startups. A technology company that had so much promise. The company developed a product for charging electrical devices wirelessly. The concept was developed by its founder while a student at the University of Pennsylvania. It basically takes ultrasound waves and focuses them at a receiver that converts the waves into electricity. (CNBC 2016). Sounds simple, right? Well there a lot of issues to work out to make uBeam's product productive and profitable.

When you develop a product and a corresponding core business model the number one thing that a company must provide is a viable product for your customer. If the product is not viable there is no way a core business model can be developed for the organization. uBeam got way ahead of itself and did not test out the viability of their product before it had raised significant seed finance.

You see, when the engineers of uBeam said they got ahead of themselves they were exactly right. (Tech Crunch 2015). It is the core business model (serving customers profitably) that defines a successful business not the product in total. It is very difficult to provide an operation for a product that does both serve customers with their needs and maintain profitable performance. This is a constant battle for most companies and is why organizations focus on business improvement performance so intensely. The balance between meeting customer needs and profitable performance will both make a product successful and an organization viable.

uBeam got too far in front of its sustainability and did not have a viable product. Every technology startup needs to clearly understand their core business model - serving customers profitably. If you don't fully understand the core, you will not follow a correct path for business priorities, goals, projects and new products. Keep focused on serving customers profitably and your organization's core business model. You will then gain reality-based business for your organization and will be successful with your initiatives. Most of all avoid, like uBeam who missing the point completely and wasting a great opportunity. It will be interesting to see when and if uBeam will display their product or is it still "want-ware". We will have to see if they have refocused and finally got their core business back on track.

Yahoo!

In 2012 Marissa Mayer had the most difficult task to turn around Yahoo Inc. She had inherited a company that had really lost its way. Yahoo once was the company to beat. It was the company that had the internet business that everyone was looking to build. Somehow Yahoo slowly day by day lost its way.

Marissa Mayer knew that Yahoo had lost its culture to innovate and needed something to fire up the core. So that same year she started a series of events to reorganize the company and attempted to reset the culture. One such event was that she gave everyone in the company an iPhone. (Business Insider 2012).

Why did Marissa Mayer give everyone at Yahoo an iPhone? Ms. Mayer knew that an iPhone embodied the innovative spirit that she was trying to get back into Yahoo. The company needed to understand who the customer is and what the market needs and wants of Yahoo's services. But, Ms. Mayer had an even bigger problem, Yahoo had no focus, goal or core business model. The market is not kind and if you don't find your core business model, serve customers and operate profitably, your company will be refactored and even sold off to other companies.

In January 2016 Yahoo announced a significant restructure. The company had the most significant reorganization and employee layoff to date. (Business Insider 2016). This major reorganization and service refit was an indication that Yahoo still had not found its core business model. Basically, they did not have an essential reason why they exist to serve their customers. It went beyond brand issues. It went beyond product issues. Yahoo needed to answer this question "why would a person or organization buy from us versus anyone else?" That was the issue that Yahoo had not resolved to that day.

Yahoo needed to understand who they were, how they could serve their customers uniquely and how they would fit into the tech market. Until they could find their core they would just be another company of product experimentations. Products melted together by trial and error in the hopes that one of their products will gain traction in the market. As it was, Yahoo was still searching for its place in the tech world. I personally was rooting for Yahoo and Ms. Mayer to figure out their core business model. I was just not sure how much time ownership would give them to pull it together.

In July 2016, we received our answer, Yahoo announced they will be broken up and sold off to other companies. A company that had the internet business that shined and was the company to beat in the internet market. Yahoo lost its way fell into confusion and had no identity in the technology world. The industry passed it by and the company could not catch up. (Forbes 2016)

If a company cannot find its core business model, how to operate from the customer perspective, they will not be successful with products, operations or improvement projects. Leadership must understand their core business model for success. Yahoo is a clear example of high-risk failure with its lack of core business model clarity.

uBeam and Yahoo, a new tech company and an older tech company, both had difficulties and both missed the center of the issue, fulfilling a core business model. Neither one could find how to serve customers with a needed product or service in a profitable on-going operation. The law of business reality cannot be escaped and for these two companies, they eventually succumbed to the lack of core business model clarity.

Core Business Model—Your Organization

When you start an improvement initiative, first think about what is your organization's core business model. If you cannot clearly articulate why your company generates profit differently from your competitors, then you have to question what is it and does our leadership know what it is. If your company is viable, then there is a core business model in operation. A question to ask leadership is "Do they know what the core business model is?" Or simply ask, "Do you know why we make money differently from our competitors?" If they cannot answer, then that is where you start your project, a basic understanding, and communication of the core business model. When that is established, then you will be able to connect basic goals and objectives with more clarity and effectiveness.

The core business model will intuitively and directly give better focus, scope, and purpose to all your improvement projects. With this connection to the core business model, improvement projects will also be easily connected to detailed goals and objectives in the short-term perspective.

But a discussion about the core business model can also be divisive and politically unpopular, especially if other management leaders are promoting something completely different. This is even truer if projects have been promoted for political gain instead of improving the organization holistically. Approach with care, especially if this is a brand-new concept that you will be introducing. But in the end, ultimately it will make your improvement project successful from all aspects.

If your project is counter to the core business model, then your project will not be successful, will not improve the enterprise, and more than likely will waste corporate resources. If your project is enabling the core business model, your project will be on good footing. Understanding the core business model and understanding how your organization generates profit by serving customers is the basic, foundational principle and is the target to which all improvement projects must start.

Business-Improvement Model

Step 1 Understand the Law of Business Reality
Organizations serve customers in a profitable way (balance quality and efficiency) or cease to exist.

Step 2 Understand the Target—The Core Business Model
The essence of the organization. Why an organization generates profit differently from its competitors.

CHAPTER 4

INFLUENCERS OF THE CORE BUSINESS MODEL

I am sure that you have heard the phrase "Build a better mousetrap." I smile every time someone says that phrase. Why? It is simple yet encompasses all the complexity and ingenuity required for new products and services. It also states the common sense that is embraced when developing new products and services. It seems so straightforward and easy. But the reality is that to develop a better mousetrap is much more complex and requires understanding of basic business elements to formulate a new "mousetrap." Without these elements, a business will not succeed or support a viable core business model. These elements are called the influencers of a core business model. These same elements or influencers are used to develop, build, improve, or even destroy a core business model in an organization.

It is important to note that an influencer is an organization entity, industry aspect, or operating environment that affects performance of the core business model. They are part of core business model viability; by themselves, influencers are not a business model. A core business model operates within a circle of influencing elements and requires influencers, or it cannot stand on its own as a viable business. But if one influencing element is overbearing, then the influencer could be so strong that it could shut down a viable business model.

To understand influencers of a core business model further, let's review the three main groups.

- **Environment**—industry, geography, governments (regulations), and competitors
- **Operation**—resources, execution, ownership, and leadership
- **Innovation**—technology, methods, and procedures

Environment

The environment influencer is the composite of external forces that affect and define the performance of a core business model. Another way to state the environmental influencer is that an organization conducts operations within an environment that consist of an industry, geography or location, government or governing entity, and competitors.

The industry environmental influencer is the trade for the organization. The industry or trade for an organization will dictate markets, processes, methods, and regulation to which a company will operate. For instance, in the commercial construction industry, an organization will most likely perform customer assessments, building designs, and land acquisition; manage subcontractors; and adhere to local zoning and codes. Also, the industry will determine operations for the front, middle, and back offices, including administration and human resource. These aspects are very common to all organizations in the construction industry and are part of the industry influencer that is present with all organizations.

The geographic, environmental influencer is the physical location of operation. The location of an organization is influenced by the local resources, accessibility, and regulations. Where an organization selects its location of operation has many positive or negative influences on execution. For instance, a trucking logistics company wants to locate its terminals near major interstates. A farmer wants accessibility to a water supply, large steel manufacturers need to be located near large shipping, and electric and gas need a power supply. Location also has governmental aspects to consider, including taxation and regulation. Geographical selection also has influence in resources or labor pools of skilled workers. The selection of operation geography is an essential influencer of an organization's core business model.

The government environmental influencer I believe is intuitive. All governments have regulation that will affect a core business model and need to be mitigated. In some industries, the government has specific governing bodies, for instances, in financial services and banking the government has the FDIC and the OCC. Some are broad based like the EPA for manufacturing, and some are self-governed like professional sports and the owners associations. On top of industry-based governing bodies, organizations are influenced by national, federal, and local governments. All these governing bodies set rules and regulations, and some perform audits to make sure that procedures are being followed. Regardless of the governing source, all organizations adhere to some level of influence by a governing body that affects a core business model's performance.

An example of government influence is obviously regulation. Government is in the business of making regulations to serve the public. By mere definition, the government is an influencer of a core business model. Regulation could affect personal habits like smoking bans in public areas or business habits like the tax reforms that prevent tax losses from being applied to other businesses. Regulation could be widespread like the government regulation of auto emissions. A word of caution: if your organization has built its core business model based on a government regulation, a change in that regulation could end your company's profitability over night.

The competitor environmental influencer is also intuitive but should be appreciably weighted. The introduction of new companies creates pressures on market share and introduces forces to which a company must perform to its core business model and the law of business reality. You can see effects of new competition every day. Whether it is a new restaurant that has opened near your neighborhood or new bank that has built a new branch in your town, competition is always on the move and changing your organization's ability to perform. Let's explore two examples of the competitive influence.

I am sure you have heard of Netflix, an organization that built on a core business model for easy transportation of video media. Netflix has become so popular that not only have Amazon and other media sources developed their own offerings, but video giants like Hollywood Video and Blockbuster have been all but put out of business. Not understanding competitive forces could quickly put an end to any viable core business model.

Another competitor influencer example is in the auto industry. In the 1920s, Ford Motor Company was the automotive force with which all other companies were trying to compete. Automobiles had been in the marketplace for some time and because of the innovation of the assembly line, Ford had a profitable company with significant market share. But General Motors had recently hired a new CEO with a grand plan to reorganize and serve customers uniquely. By making design modifications every year, GM would make cars more attractive to first-time buyers. With that change, GM was able to surpass Ford in market share, a status that would not change until 2009. Competition is a great influencer that cannot be ignored within an organization's operating environment.

I am sure that you have examples and stories as well. To be sure, competition is a great influencer and should be used to hone your organization's core business model threats. But one aspect of competition is still the law of business reality: serve your customers in a profitable way. Keep focused on customers rather than competition. I have seen companies fixated on competition and not performance for customers. That will be the quickest way to destroy a core business model. So make sure you keep an appropriate level on competition but focus on your customers.

Operation

Operation is at the heart of an organization. It is the most visible and tangible evidence of a working company. More specifically, operation is when an organization brings to bear resources, functions, strategy, execution, and efficiency to serve its customers profitably. You see, the organization uses assets (whether tangible or intangible) to fulfill its core business model, and assets are utilized to execute a strategy, to realize a profitable operation. Assets are very expensive, and unless an organization enables them to achieve its core business model operation, a company will take a fast track to Chapter 11 bankruptcy. There are three parts to an operation that all need to work together to generate a profitable organization. These major components are categorized as resources, execution, and leadership.

Resources

Resources are the sources of working elements to produce services or deliver products (e.g., raw materials, human capital, and technology systems). The formulation of resources is a key component to forming a profitable organization. Without the right or alignment of resources, an organization will not perform to its ability regardless of how good a core business model looks on paper. The acquiring of quality resources, whether it is people, materials, or suppliers, must be achieved to produce a quality product or service. A great teacher of leadership once said you need to find the right people to get on the bus before you know where you are going. Why? Because you need the right people to help determine your direction before the bus can leave the station.

Have you ever been in an organization where you're not sure the direction of the company? That is just the point. Picking the wrong people can lead to disunity, destructive competition, and even fraud—all of which can destroy a core business model and send a company into dissolution. The first priority is selecting the right people, because people are the first enabler to a core business model of an organization.

Just like selecting the right people, selecting quality raw materials is paramount. You know the saying "Garbage in, garbage out." Usually, the term is used when speaking about decisions or technology systems. But it holds true for operations as well. When you select ingredients, raw resources, or materials that are lower quality, then you can expect lower-quality products. Unless your process is to improve the lower-quality resources, you will not improve anything but selecting lower-quality materials. The product by definition will be of lower quality.

This goes directly to the law of business reality. Lowering costs is a good and needed approach to improving an organization's profitability, but if the quality is not to the expectations of your customer, then you will lose customers and sales. Cheaper resources might be good for the short term, but your organization might be sacrificing short-term profits and long-term viability. When approaching selecting resources, make sure you are not breaking your organization's core business model with inferior resources of any kind.

Execution

Execution is the ability of an organization to utilize resources to a profitable end (fulfill the law of business reality). Quality resources are required to building a quality product or service just as quality logistics (execution) is required for a profitable operation. Here is where processes, resources, and technology all come together to steer the organization's core process to a profitable end. Sound familiar? It should. This is where the law of business reality with the core business model will be fulfilled in full force. Execution is also where the most obvious showing of organizational quality will be evidenced for a customer.

There are many aspects of execution that are considered in business improvement. We will be covering some of these aspects in other sections (i.e., business processes), but in this section, we are concerned with the core business model execution influence to support or resist change for an organization's ability to move to a preferable state of performance.

It is change influence, or more accurately change resistance, that is at the core of the execution influence. How an organization's current processes are entrenched in the current operation has a lot to do with the organization's ability to change as much as the culture's will to change. A company must be able to change itself. Why? Because everything around the company is changing constantly. The ability to make changes and keep pace with outside influencers is a major component of execution agility and profitability. If a company is unwilling to modify its current processes, it will miss a major point of the law of business reality and be on a road to company destruction.

I was with a company in a business-improvement department where the culture actually perpetuated resistance to change. I was assigned to project after project where every time an improvement was put to a business case, one of the business leaders was able to stop the project or filibuster long enough to stall out the momentum. Eventually, the company hit an economic downturn and its ability to change was so foreign that the company went into change shock. This happens when a company needs to change fast to meet the demands of a shift in market but leadership goes into confusion and starts to misinterpret the real change that needs to be performed. The company's performance was not hidden. Wall Street exposed its performance issues with a stock price well below its peers. This company needed a change in leadership before it could perform real business improvement and change to its operations.

Ownership

Ownership refers to the owners of the company. They have the final decision in any company. Since ownership is directly tied to legal responsibility, this influencer has a double impact. Ownership hires leadership to run the company. Sometimes, it is one in the same; nonetheless, the ownership has ultimate influence in how the company is run.

In publicly traded companies, this is an equally understood aspect. The board of directors for a public company will hire a CEO to run the company but the CEO might not have the same amount of ownership. That means the CEO will get directions from the board of directors. Each time, the CEO will make his or her "pitch" on how to run the company, but the ownership has the ultimate say within the company. They can make the ultimate decision to continue operations, sell, merge, or even cease operating the company. One cannot underestimate the ultimate influence of the ownership and its influence on the operation of the company.

Leadership

When defining leadership, one can find many definitions, resources, and examples including writings from Peter Drucker, Tom Peters, and the leader in leadership training, John Maxwell. But leadership, when defining the influencers of a business model, is much more defined and finite. Leadership, for this section, is the company's ability to strategize and produce sound decisions to further a core business model.

This goes without question. Leaders must be acutely aware of the dangers of making the wrong decision. The organization's leadership and its ability to understand markets, measures, and execution will be judged every day, as it will produce a favorable outcome or dissolution. Leaders must have the insight and resolution to pursue the right decision even in the face of opposition.

You don't need to look far for an example of the influence of operational leadership as in Jack Welch. Operation is the basis for profitable organizations. Based on my understanding of the facts, when Jack took over for GE, he instinctively knew that the company needed to focus on what it did well, and if it could not do first or second in a market, he got rid of the division. He understood the influence of leadership in operation. He mustered his resources, focused them into segments that would gain operational performance, and exited those that would not generate industry-leading profits. Needless to say, GE became a performance giant because Jack Welch understood the influence of operational leadership.

This kind of perseverance is not limited to business. You see it in leaders like Winston Churchill, Thomas Edison, George Washington, Abraham Lincoln, etc. In the face of defeat, they were steadfast in their position and did what was right for their country or organization. They could break down politics and obstacles and keep focused on the vision to the end—to success.

Needless to say, operational excellence is a must for performing organizations. But it is the leadership that stands in the gap to drive that operational performance. Without the leadership to develop new strategies and interpret the core business model influencers, a company has no hope of surviving external and internal pressures that will eventually destroy its own operational core business model. When initiating an improvement project, it is imperative to identify leadership that will understand this important aspect and drive new improvements. Without operational leadership support, you will be wasting valuable resources that could be utilized in a more productive initiative.

Innovation

Now we get to the most critical influencer, at least for this book: innovation. Innovation is the company's ability to utilize technology, methods, or procedures to improve its operation. A new technology, process method, or updated procedure can drive innovation and discover a new way of developing products, improving business process, or enabling pioneering operations. These innovations can drive new business models, start new ventures, or even revamp existing companies. Innovation drives companies to remain competitive within their industry and market. Technology as an influencer is so significant that an entire chapter is devoted to technology resource for an organization's core business model and business improvement.

I have not heard of a single person, business, organization, or government for that matter that improved without innovation. Think about it. In countries throughout history, governments have risen and fallen because other countries with better technology and innovation have made better war machines. Most wars (or conflicts) have been won with better leadership and better innovation.

In an organization, innovation is the catalyst for improvement, and for some, it is the transformation to a new business altogether. You can find great examples in history, from the innovation of the cotton gin to electricity, automobile, space flight, cell phones, and the Internet. Innovation has changed the way we perform business operations and continue to shape business improvement to anyone who will embrace a new technology to change their existing organization or create new ones.

I learned a great example of innovation from many personal visits to a small mill in western Pennsylvania. In 1868, a small gristmill on the Slippery Rock River burned to the ground. It was rebuilt in 1875 by Thomas McConnell, who became a great innovator for his time. You see, in the 1870s, it took five people three days to mill a wagon full of wheat into flour. And if you had other grain to mill, you had to wait until one set of grain was completed before you could mill a different grain.

At McConnell's mill, they had the same power source that most mills used: water. But when Thomas McConnell rebuilt the mill, he harnessed a new power accelerator called a water turbine that generated greater torque and speed than current water paddle mills. With this power source, plus adding rolling mills instead of grindstones, Thomas McConnell built a new operation that included grain shoots, conveyers, sifters, and collectors. A marvel for its time.

With this innovation, McConnell's mill was able to process a wagon full of grain in hours with one operator. And if you had multiple grains to mill, the operation had weights and lifters that guided different kinds of grains to separate shoots for processing. This innovation was leveraged to gain a 500 percent productivity and 300 percent time savings. The fact that the water was free also made the only significant cost a "technician" to maintain the machinery. Even though the flour produced is relatively the same, the process to produce the flour had significant innovation improvements, which increased productivity. This innovation set up McConnell's mill as the leading mill on the river for the next forty years. A simple innovation of a water turbine changed the way grains were processed forever and had significant effects on organizations and other millers in the Slippery Rock valley. Innovation influence is a game changer in an industry for business improvement. Innovation can even set up a new core business model (On Site Sources at McConnell's Mill n.d.).

Innovation is also an influencer wildcard. A company could under innovate or in some cases over-innovate. How much of it and the right fit of innovation is a key to a successful improvement. I have seen companies try to implement large technology projects just to discover that the innovation was not appropriate for its operation or industry. Some projects I have seen destroy companies because the technology was so expensive it took all available resources to implement and left the company with very limited operating capital. In some of those cases, although extreme, the project actually was the element that drove the business into bankruptcy. Innovation needs to be measured against an organization's ability to digest significant changes. Otherwise, it will have the opposite effect and even lead to the demise of a company.

This also means even more outside innovation that is developed could change or introduce new products or competitors into the market. Technology innovation could also change major methods and efficacies for an industry which we will cover in a succeeding section. Innovation is a key element in determining a working core business model and is influenced by other influencers in the environment and a company's current operation. The same influencers that create a new business model are also the forces that are constantly causing pressure to destroying one.

It is the three together that influence a core business model's performance and are the key components when reviewing and taking the first steps in improving an organization. Ignoring these influencers will send your organization into an early death. Leveraging them can build an organization that is built to sustain performance for years.

Core Business Models and Influencers

How is a core business model developed? Taking the entrepreneurial viewpoint, a need or problem is identified in the market that is not being economically fulfilled. The need or problem is filtered through environmental considerations, innovation aspects, and operational strategies to create a concept of a new business model that addresses the need or problem. A core business model is then tested for business viability and then deployed into market operation. A new company is started and the core business model is in operation. In a sense, we have built a better mousetrap.

But in order to build a better mousetrap, you must also build an organization along with a better core business model to support the new mousetrap. You see, a poorly conceived core business model, a poorly executed operation, or underestimating environmental or innovation aspects can destroy an organization. All core business model influencers must be considered and interpreted to the total improvement. It is unfair, but it is reality, that any one aspect of the influencers interpreted inaccurately can sink the entire project. And all influencers must be interpreted accurately to be successful.

It is also a note of influence impact that the process of formalization of resources and influencers into a viable core business model is the process known as operationalization. A core business model is worthless unless it can be realized. The real aspect is this: can a core business model be operationalized or can it be turned into a profitable operation?

Sometimes, this is also referred to as simply "Is it a profitable business?" Many times, core business model influencers are not fully understood until an attempt is made to operationalize the model. It is also at that time where many businesses fail due to lack of understanding.

A core business model is always being attacked because business is always in motion and influencers are always changing. In fact, in the same way influencers are used to formulate business models, they can also destroy them. Another phrase you most likely have heard of is "We do not use buggy whips anymore." At one time, there were blacksmiths and buggy whip manufacturers when horse-drawn carriages were the main source for ground transportation. Eventually, innovations developed and the automobile took over as the main source for ground transportation. Buggy whip companies needed to transform, or they went out of business.

Influencers will influence other influencers. This simply means that influencers are not completely independent of each other. Each influencer has components that are either dependent or connected to each other. For instance, as part of the environment influencer, the industry influencer will determine a majority of operation for an organization. As has been detailed in the operation influencer, the industry dictates a framework of functions and processes and sets in motion many of the performance foundations. It is the imprint of the industry environment that will form the basis for operations and in many cases form the foundation for process automation. These industry influencers include manufacturing, service, financial service, retail, wholesale, and energy. We will review the industry influencer more fully in the industry process section.

The next and almost as important aspect to the core business model is the business influencers. Influencers are critical to the success of any business-improvement project. They are not separate or independent of improvement and pose a major impact as projects target benefit and success. One should ask, "What is the environment, the operation, and innovation that will be used in conjunction with the improvement initiative?" Answer those questions and you will begin to understand the forces on your improvement project that will perform to plan, budget, and performance targets.

Business Improvement Model

Step 1 Understand the Law of Business Reality
Organizations serve customers in a profitable way (balance quality and efficiency) or cease to exist.

Step 2 Understand the Target—The Core Business Model
Why organizations generate profit different from their competitors.

Step 3 Influencers of the Core Business Model
Pressure and Enhancers on Performance

CHAPTER 5

THE LAW, CORE, AND INFLUENCE— BUSINESS STRATEGY AND STRUCTURE

To this point, we have reviewed the basics of an organization and strategy for operations. We have covered the law of business reality, where a company must serve customers profitably. We have also reviewed centric to all profitable organizations the core business model which makes them not only unique but also makes an organization profitable and separates it from its competitors. Then we reviewed the last component in this group, which is the core business model influencers that applies performance pressure and enhancers of a core business model and can even create or destroy an entire business model. But a question we need to ask is this: how do all of these work together?

These three—the law, the core, and the influencers—represent an organization's business strategy structure. Meaning the law, core, and influencers together form the basis for business strategy to which a company goes to market. Before any improvement project is developed, conceived, formularized, or embarked upon, the strategy structure, as outlined here as the law, core, and the influencers, must be strategized as a single model. If not, then stop the project because your improvement project is 50 percent dead before it even starts. How and why?

In studying and participating in numerous improvement projects, the issues all point back to this single issue. The project leadership did not understand basic profitability, core process operation, or an influencing element, which are all part of a bigger issue of the core business model and influencers. Missing this element will adversely affect a project and cause the project to miss planned delivery value or iterate until resources are exhausted to the point of project shutdown.

Why? The point is simple. The law, core, and influencers are what make a company work profitably. If your project does not embrace business strategy as the law, the core, or the influencers, then the leadership will instinctively push back on the project. Business leaders are neither ignorant nor *stupid*. They are either overt or covert leaders, but they all are aware of profitability and they all are knowledgeable about what will generate profitable benefit.

All projects must start with a clear understanding of architecting the business strategy. Here it is understood as the composite agreement among the law, core, and influencers to a profitable end. But sometimes, even the business leaders cannot articulate business strategy and structure clearly. Let me explain business strategy first using the following diagram:

Business Strategy Development

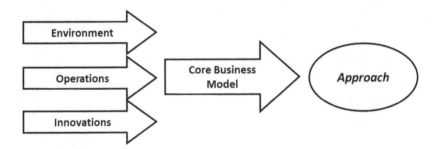

Typically, an organization, whether it is a ten-, five-, or one-year plan, goes through a process to determine an approach. The approach can be represented in different terms. Sometimes, it is called the "go to market" plan or "operation" plan, or sometimes the "strategy" or simply the "goals and objectives" of an organization for a specific duration. No matter the term for the company, it is articulating the result of filtering and analyzing the influencers on the core business model to a planned approach for performance. This process is normally called business strategy development. The main output from the business strategy development is an approach and the structure of the business strategy is called the business strategy structure, which embraces the law, core, and influencers to a profitable approach.

For improvement professionals, it is *not* your responsibility to develop a business strategy that is clearly in the hands of executive leadership. It *is* your responsibility to *clearly* understand aspects of the business strategy and how it relates to your improvement initiative. As mentioned before, sometimes leadership does not clearly articulate business strategy (approach) as it relates to a core business model, but as a business-improvement professional, it *is your* responsibility to understand the relationship. Business-improvement projects must start with a clear linkage to what they are trying to improve and how it embraces business strategy and structure.

To establish a clear understanding and linkage between the improvement initiative and business strategy (approach), it can be a simple process. Just ask, "How does this approach improve the organization's core business model?" If you cannot answer this question in real terms, then your project is already in jeopardy. You must find the linkage by researching the relationship between the improvement initiative and the business strategy structure or the resulting approach. If you can make a clear linkage, then you are on the best track for a business-improvement initiative and the linkage will carry throughout the project's life cycle. If you cannot reconcile the linkage, then you must question the initiative's validity. It is better to question the validity of a project before it starts than to begin and fail to perform.

There are many examples of broken linkage projects and how they eventually failed to perform or stopped completely. In the late 1990s when year 2000 projects were numerous, many companies were implementing ERP or enterprise resource planning packages. The business case was simply stating that if a company needs to spend X dollars on upgrading all systems for year 2000 compliant, why not invest that capital into a brand-new innovation of process and technology in an ERP? Although each company that used this business case had good intentions, you can clearly see that this reason to implement an enterprise,base system did not consider an organization's current business strategy or enable a core business model. Implementing technology for technology sake will fail every time. This was indicative of the implementation failure rate in the late 1990s, which was at an all-time high.

One such company whose implementation highlighted this situation was AmeriServe. I learned of its situation firsthand when I served as an expert witness. AmeriServe supplied food to the QSR or quick service restaurant industry, mostly known for servicing fast-food franchised restaurants like Burger King, Taco Bell, KFC, etc. The company was a wholesaler and distributor of food items that QSRs used in meal preparation. AmeriServe had a high-volume, just-in-time service with a low-margin business model. The company, like most in the late 1990s, needed to make its software systems year 2000 compliant. It was persuaded by outside consultants to implement an ERP instead of upgrading its current systems to be year 2000 compliant.

The AmeriServe project started with all the right elements of a quality project. But soon after the implementation began, the consulting teams found many issues with matching the software functionality and AmeriServe business operation. The team spent large amounts of resources trying to make the functionality run the business. After years of implementing by reducing scope, adding resources, and switching consulting firms, the team finally had an operating system for the company.

A short time after the system went into production operation, the company began to miss SLAs (service level agreements) with its QSR customers. Then the company began to miss deliveries completely because the software ran the organization more closely to a logistical trucking company than AmeriServe's QSR process food distribution company. The company began to lose customers and eventually the system caused so much nonperformance that AmeriServe filed for bankruptcy.

It is hard to believe a project that was intended to improve the business did just the opposite. The implementation team had a misinterpretation of improvement linkage with business strategy or even the core business model which drove AmeriServe to cease operation. But this is the danger that can happen to every business-improvement project. The linkage between the business strategy structure (the law, core, and influencer with the approach) and improvement projects is the center of improvement success, and in the case of AmeriServe, it was the difference between success and insolvency.

I am willing to bet that you have heard of a few examples of projects that failed. Anyone that has been in the industry for a decade has been familiar with an innovation, improvement, or technology project that has missed its goals. Review these projects and analyze based on these three elements. See if you can uncover which element was underestimated or missed completely, and I am sure that you will find the source of the project failure. The following table highlights examples:

Examples of Broken Linkage Projects

Project Aspect	Control	Benefit	Linkage Resolved
Funding	LOB Sponsored	Enterprise Benefit	Enterprise Sponsored
Support	Committee	Specific LOB Funding	Committee Funded
Vision	Enterprise Wide	Individual LOB Contributed	Enterprise Contributed
Enablement	IT Lead	Business Process	Business Lead

This table highlights symptoms of a project that has broken linkage in respect to its core business model support. If your initiative falls into one of these groups, you should step back and make an analysis of what the project is trying to improve. These symptoms will not go away. These aspects will be deeply rooted and may not manifest their broken linkage until the project has started or even further down the implementation cycle. Not reconciling the broken linkage will cause the project to iterate and falter until eventually the initiative will fail completely. Your project cannot escape this fact. You must deal with broken linkage or you will incur faulty or fake improvement. If your organization overlooks or even hides the broken linkage, then your organization will suffer the same fate as AmeriServe, a broken enablement that will cause business model insolvency.

If all you get out of this book is to understand how important implementing to improve the core business model is, then you have gotten the gist of the reality of business improvement. When you start an improvement project, start with a blank page and see if you can articulate your organization's core business model and influencers that will affect your project's performance. If you can list them, then verify with top leaders. If you cannot, then there is some work to be done to gain understanding for your organization.

Once you can clearly articulate the core business model and influencers (the business strategy of the organization), then you can compare to your own project benefits. If the linkage is at all unclear, then step back and find out why. Do not start a project until linkage is clear or your project will be part of the statistics of failed projects stated in the beginning of this book. If the linkage is clear, then your project has good footing on which to start the project and has the start of an all-around successful business-improvement initiative.

Business Strategy Section Reprise

Business strategy is the understanding of how the law, core, and influences together produce a workable model, and the structure for implementation is the structure that is implored. Each project must first understand each aspect of the strategy and then filter through the structure to make the connection for improvement. If the linkage is clear, then proceed. If not, go back and review aspects of the improvement to make sure that real improvement is targeted for attainment.

With the conclusion of this section on business strategy structure, I wanted to make sure it is clear that it is the law, core, and influencers together that make a business "work" and perform. The strategy is just that, a strategy that proves itself everyday by profitable performance. A successful organization is one that can serve its customers every day and maintain profitability. It is not because an operational concept has been perfected in an Excel worksheet. It is the resolve and durability of an actual business that has successfully met its customers' needs.

So when you approach an improvement project, if your company has performed profitably for many years, then it is to be respected and even honored. There is a reason why the company has passed the test of durability with year over year sustainability. That reason could also be a key to unlocking a core business model of culture. A core business model of culture is a company that understands itself so well that it is woven into the culture. That kind of company is to be envied and modeled as it has its customers and organization in focus for the highest performance.

Business-Improvement Model

Part 1: Business Strategy Structure

Step 1 Understand the Law of Business Reality
Organizations serve customers in a profitable way (balance quality and efficiency) or cease to exist.

Step 2 Understand the Target—The Core Business Model
Why organizations generate profit different from their competitors.

Step 3 Influencers of the Core Business Model
Pressure and Enhancers on Performance

Step 4 Embrace Core Model—Business Strategy Structure
Basis for Improvement—Whether Leaders Know It or Not

PART 2

BUSINESS OPERATION—THE BUSINESS PROCESS STRUCTURE

Section Introduction

In this section, we will explore the relationship between the core business model and business process. It may surprise you that the connection is so direct and specific, but the connection is essential to business process structure for the entire organization. It is not necessarily what you may have learned in the past, but it is the basis for sound understanding of enterprise performance. Let's begin core business model based business process structure.

CHAPTER 6

THE BUSINESS—BASIS FOR FUNCTIONS AND PROCESS

Where do processes come from? Have you noticed in process improvement projects we always start with the basic assumption of knowing a business process? That is, we can define what a business process is and how it is used in our organization. In fact, we can find many industry-based definitions of a business process.

> A business process or business method is a collection of related, structured activities or tasks that produce a specific service or product (serve a particular goal) for a particular customer or customers. (*Wikipedia* n.d.)

> A business process is an activity or set of activities that will accomplish a specific organizational goal. (Rouse n.d.)

> Series of logically related activities or tasks (such as planning, production, sales) performed together to produce a defined set of results. *(Business Dictionary* n.d.)

All these definitions point to the same concept—a business process is a set of actions that take place to fulfill a vision, goal, or product/service. But have you ever asked, "Where do these processes come from?" I asked that same question of some of my improvement colleagues and it stopped them dead in their tracks. They had a thoughtful moment and paused to contemplate the question. They knew if they said nothing, they would appear unwise, but if they said the obvious, they would appear obviously unwise. So they answered honestly and said, "Are not processes inherent to a business?"

Actually, their gut reaction was a true and honest answer. The answer is *yes*, processes are inherent to any business, and business processes are how a business really works. I asked some of my technology colleagues to describe how a business works, and I asked the same question to some of my business colleagues in a large corporation. The response was basically the same. They both easily could explain how their department fit in the organization, but neither of them could tell me how their entire company works together. Sad but true. Many of us simply do not know how an organization *works* in total.

But to understand how a business works, we must answer the question "Where do processes come from?" Or more directly, "Where is the business process inherited from?" Why? Because how an organization works and business process inheritance are symbiotic. Let's refer to our definition: a business process (sometimes referred to as organizational process) is the set of actions that take place for an organization to fulfill its vision profitable. If you think this definition sounds like the law of business reality, you are not far off. When fulfilling an organization's core business model, a company performs functions and processes based on first the law of business reality and second an organization's core business model.

The reality is that total enterprise business process is the total operation of fulfilling the core business model. This is also why it is sometimes referred to as the "composite functional execution" of the core business model. Basically, business process gets its foundation from first the law of business reality and second from the operation of an organization's core business model. That is why business processes are inherent to a business; otherwise, an organization would not perform business functions to serve customers in a profitable way. So business processes come from the operation to perform functions to serve customers uniquely in a profitable way.

Business processes are the functional operations needed to uniquely serve customers in a profitable way.

Organizational Functions and Processes

In the previous section, we alluded to a relationship between functions and business processes. In fact, there is a direct relationship that is also the foundation for operational performance. To understand this relationship, we must first define business functions and then how they relate to business processes.

A business *function* is the individual goal required to achieve a larger business goal (the core business model). An organization based on business models has many business functions that need to be performed. Each goal is subdivided into small goals which then are translated into smaller, executable components called functions. These smaller, executable components are the most basic goals of an organization and represent the total functional operation of an organization. Some differences to functions and process include the following:

> A function is a set of business activities that does not have a finite start and endpoint. The function is generally an ongoing effort within a company.

> A process is a business activity which does have a finite start and endpoint. Processes are generally a lower level construct of an operation.

We have previously described what business process and functions represent but what is the relationship between a business process and a business function? A business process is a series of steps required to achieve a business function. So in a sense, the function is *what* needs to be accomplished and the process is *how* the function is to be accomplished. When we say that a process needs to be functional, we are saying that the process needs to achieve its specific business goal for that process. Remember the business function is the smallest executable and achievable goal that can be performed and the process is the means by which the function is to be performed.

An example can be found in a simple cell phone display. If a cell phone needs to be able to display different time zones (the functional goal), then the steps to achieve the display of different time zones is called the process. The function and process distinction is depicted in the following diagram:

Business Functions and Process Relationship

Time Zones	Display Time Zones

Function – Business goals to perform. The "what" to perform.   *Process – Steps to perform the function. The "how" to perform.*

The business process is the execution of functional components, which is termed "functional execution." When we look at the entire organization, this total collection of business process executes a series of steps that represents all the operational functionality of the company or the "composite functional execution" of the organization.

Now that we understand business functions and processes, what is the basis for business process performance? Business process performance in general is identified by the dependent relationship between a business function and a business process. The relationship is highlighted by two factors: process efficiency and functionality achieved.

Since the role of process is to execute a business function, then the performance is measured on how efficiently the process is executing the business functionality and how well the business functionality is being achieved. This measurement can also be stated in a question. "Is the process functional and efficient?" This is a quick way to state a functional and process performance that is ultimately achieved and supported by an organization's core business model.

In this section, we will just mention the efficiency and functionality measurements in general terms. Later, we will explore a more calculated measurement that includes a concept of productivity. For these purposes, the efficiency measurement is measured by the question "Does the process perform the function with least amount of steps and time?" The functionality measurement is measured by the goal achievement, which is based on the core business model and the law of business reality.

For one to understand functional and process performance measurement, we must first ask, "What do we compare the performance measurement against?" Many improvement projects miss true business performance; hence, performance measurement is wrongly linked. In fact, some of my colleagues fail to understand how to drive true enterprise performance. To resolve this elusive question of measurement, we must first understand *common* enterprise functions and processes.

Common Organizational Functions and Processes

Based on the law of business reality, there are basic *functions* which every organization must perform by definition of a profitable business. These basic or common functions are based on the major business purposes for a profitable organization. Each of these major purposes has separate goals that work together systematically for a profitable operation. Without these major functions working together, the company would be in danger of working outside the law and eventually lead to dissolution. These major functional goals can be divided into three distinct major functions for an organization here described as

1. a way to communicate,
2. a way to develop or deliver a product or service, and
3. a way to administrate a product or service for your customers.

Let's review these three major functions.

First, every organization must have a way of communicating its existence and how it uniquely will serve its customers. This type of communication to an individual person or organization is referred to as the marketing function. Without communicating an organization's existence, a potential customer will not be aware of the provided product or service. From the communication, this is a natural extension to retain a customer to purchase the product or service. This function is commonly referred to as the sales function, and it is to secure or obtain the sale of a product or service from a customer.

Second, every organization must be able to produce, deliver, and service what a customer has been sold with quality and cost effectiveness. An organization must be able to produce a product or service with a competitive cost structure and deliver in a matter that meets the needs of its customers. An organization can have the best marketing and sales, but if it cannot produce the product with quality and efficiency, the organization will eventually fail in performance. This function is commonly called the development and delivery of a product or service.

Third, every organization needs to administer its internal support for the enterprise, including financials, human resources, and legal and governmental compliances. Without proper administration of cash flow management, tax and financial reporting, or government compliance reporting, an organization will not be able to manage itself and will incur sanctions, capital issues, lawsuits, or much more administrative issues. This is commonly called the administration/compliances function and supports the operation in reporting, acquiring, and performance monitoring for enterprise.

These three major functions are the common business functions that all profitable organizations perform: marketing/sales, production/delivery, and administration/compliance.

Law of Business Reality
Common Business Functions

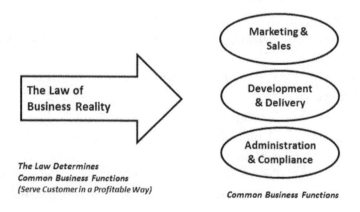

The Law of Business Reality

Marketing & Sales

Development & Delivery

Administration & Compliance

The Law Determines
Common Business Functions
(Serve Customer in a Profitable Way)

Common Business Functions

These three common functional groups are the functional basis for all organizations. Each company must have a component from each function to perform. Look at your own company. Can you identify each functional group? If you cannot, then some homework needs to be done, because if your organization is sustainable, then each of these functions, whether overt or covert, has these groups in operation. For a business-improvement professional, it is essential for you to understand the common business functions of an organization.

Common Functions Link to Common Processes

Let's review the relationship of functions and processes. The major function of an organization is *what* to perform and process is *how* these functions get performed. Since business process is based on the law of business reality, then business process is the execution of functional steps to achieve the law. That would indicate that major business processes for an enterprise would parallel major business functions of an organization, and that is true.

If this was not the case, then major functions would be out of sequence or out of alignment with business process. That would be correct. There would be huge misalignment in business process if functions were performing outside of its main functional area. You see, a business process is characterized by the functions that are being performed by the process itself.

Can you imagine if the administrative organization was trying to perform sales functions or if the product development organization was performing contract negotiating or even legal reporting? Sounds ridiculous, but that is to make a point. There is a group of specialization of functions and a sequence that parallels process groups that perform each task. But if these function groups are misaligned with their associated process groups, then there would be disorder and even chaos in operations.

We would conclude that major functions of an organization do parallel major business processes. These major businesses processes would also parallel the major functions which are denoted as marketing/sales, product/service, and administration. Both the functions and processes have common goals and steps that have already been determined by definition of the law and the organization's core business model.

The common business processes and interconnections are displayed in the following chart:

The Law of Business Reality
Common Business Processes

Goal – Communicate and obtain a sale of a product or Service for a customer

Marketing / Sales

Product / Service

Goal – Develop and delivery of a product or service with quality and cost effectives to a customer

Admin

Goal – Support the operation in legal, financial management, performance monitoring, reporting for a product or service to the customer

Every organization that serves customers and maintains its existence with fiscal responsibility has these three types of processes. One may ask, "Do nonprofit or not-for-profit organizations have these types as well?" If your organization requires a customer to pay for your products or services, then the answer is yes, you have these common processes in operation.

As stated before, the goal of marketing/sales includes the steps to acquire a new customer. Marketing in many organizations is the action to gain awareness in the marketplace to potential customers. Sales are the connection of the potential customers to acquiring an actual product or service. There are common processes to each of these areas regardless of what industry or profit status. For example, every organization needs to perform some sort of awareness to the potential customers like advertising, referrals, or simple networking. In any such industry, these actions must take place for a potential customer to acquire the organization's product or services. These steps are the common marketing and sales processes to acquire a customer sale.

Product/service process is all processes that are required to develop and administer the organization's main product or service to its customer. Whether the organization is a service company like in the financial industry or a product company like an automotive manufacturer, there are processes that are required to develop and deliver the main product or service to the customer. Whether it is a service company that delivers through the Internet or a product company that uses a trucking delivery system, all these steps are required to develop and deliver a product of service to an end customer.

Administration is simply the processes to support the operation of the enterprise. These processes include any financial transaction including cash flow, accounting, auditing, human resources, and procurement. These processes do not directly contribute to the main product or service but are needed to support functions of the enterprise and indirectly support the product or service. Even the main innovation or IT departments are usually categorized in this area. This is an area which needs understanding that it is a support function.

> **All business processes will fall under one of these major functions of an organization: marketing/sales, product/service, and administration.**

Even though this section sounded like we repeated the same concepts, we actually mirrored that major functions should parallel major processes. Marketing and sales functions should be performed in the marketing and sales processes. This is really a concept of functional alignment. Functional alignment is placing functional steps in the appropriate process step to achieve the best functional goal for the organization.

That is why when we look at a major process group, we are also talking about a major functional group. At the highest level, these processes and functions are completely in parallel. From the common process perspective, there are two other aspects that need to be to clearly understood: process interconnection and integration.

Process Interconnection

In the previous chart, the three common processes overlap in the center. This represents common business processes that overlap or are interconnected. For instance, when a sales transaction is determining which products or services are best for a customer, there are processes that might be considered sales and there are some processes that might be considered product or service. Since a company must match customers to product and service offerings, there is an overlap to which both process groups are required to resolve execution. These processes are interconnected, shared, and depend on each other for completion.

Interconnected business processes share business functions. This is a statement of fact. If a business process is shared, then the functions are shared. Sales might think they own a "product selection" process, but they do not own the product specification. Features are developed and maintained by a product management group even though the same process and function would be executed in the sales area. These shared functions can add a lot of problems to an organization by way of who owns the business process. Since most organizational structures are defined based on a finite function, shared function is owned either by all or none. This creates major process turf battles and is a source for conflict in the organization.

I think you can clearly see where interconnected business process would be the cause of conflict in an organization, since most organizations have a line of control, meaning each organization's departments have an area of responsibility. These responsibilities will overlap because enterprise processes are interconnected to perform enterprise functions. But many departments are not defined with clear areas of delineation that are tied to process responsibilities across the enterprise. This is the source of much conflict among departmental areas. Compound this with perceived performance, goals, and even incentive compensation, a natural competition develops among departments and conflict will occur.

Sometimes, it is hard to see who should own the business function and process. What is clear between shared functions and business process is these overlaps occur and, as an improvement professional,

56

you must identify these process overlaps and who will ultimately be responsible for functional and process identification and performance.

These areas are pockets for improvement and have an extra focus on handing off process performance for each group. Handing off a process execution from one area of responsibility to another is where changes occur in process enablement, methods, and management understanding of execution. These differences will cause suboptimal performance and should be an area of focus for improvement initiatives. How well these processes are integrated can either generate or detract from organizational productivity and overall performance.

Just as there is process interconnection, there is end-to-end process connection. We discussed "composite execution" as the integrated steps to achieve the major business functions of an organization. End-to-end business process is actually a single product or service that is executed throughout the organization. It is a single version of a process that encompasses the entire enterprise. This is an area in process improvement that is of great misconception. An end-to-end has many influencers and factors, but one aspect that is the most important is that an end-to-end process is customer centric.

End-to-end processes are customer centric because it is what the customer sees from the outside looking in at the company. A customer sees every interaction with a company without departmental boundaries. Think about it. A customer does not care if they are interacting with a special customer service department or the vice president of operations. They just see their need and want it fulfilled. An end-to end-process will give a lens on what a customer sees and the effects on performance with a customer. This customer interaction with the company leads us to another aspect of process that is process integration.

Process Integration

All organizations operate within a unique environment. This environment is defined by their industry, product, and customers the company serves as described by the environment influencer. Inherent in every company are interactions with an operating environment.

These interactions are represented by communications with outside organizations in order to facilitate operations. These connections with outside organizations are defined as process integrations.

With process integration, there are boundaries to and from an organization. Each boundary is determined by the operation line between the organization and the operating environment. Operations that reach outside the organization across the environment must integrate with an external business process of another organization. Process integration occurs when internal business processes connect with external process operations from another organization.

An example of process integration is when third-party sales affiliates, transportation services, payroll services, and sometimes attorneys are interacting with the organization. The organization has delegated operations and performance to an outside organization which, in turn, performs operations on behalf of the parent organization.

As depicted on the process chart, the integrated processes operate in the operating environment. Just like process interconnection, there are handoffs to other outside organizations that cross not only functional areas but other organizations completely. Also just like process interconnection, there is a broken functionality and efficiency and is a source for identified improvement. This also is where many contemporary improvement methodologies focus their attention on areas for improvement. We also identify the linkage to enterprise value as linkage to fulfilling functional business goals in and out of the enterprise.

Common Business Process
Internal and External Process Integration

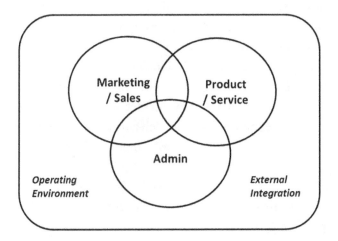

The key idea here is that anytime you delegate operation outside, you are also handing off the management of process performance. If the interaction to manage a delegated process to an outside firm is more costly than the total internal management, then it is better to perform the business process internally.

Many outsourced business processes fail at this basic principle. Before the organization can identify that the total cost of ownership for outsourcing a business process has exceeded its ability to manage the process cost effectively, the organization has spent millions of capital in the transition to an outsource organization. Before you embark on "giving up" a business process to the management of another organization, measure and simulate all the management and costs to understand the total cost of delegation.

Process and Functions Recap

This chapter covered a lot of information, but it is the basis for business process. Let's review this chapter on common business processes. First, we discovered that business processes are inherent to any business as a result of having a working core business model derived from the law of business reality. We also covered that there are a set of common business processes that perform common business functions to fulfill the core business model and are categorized into three areas: marketing/sales, product/service, and administration. Business functions and business processes parallel operation as marketing/sales, development/delivery, and administration/compliance. Business process performs business functions and their relationship is directly tied to business performance. Business processes have interconnections within the organization and the organization interacts with outside organizations called process integrations. When delegating business process to an outside organization, a company has relinquished performance control to the outside organization.

The major takeaway from this chapter is that all business processes are inherent to an organization's core business model. To operate a business profitably, there are common business processes and functions in three main areas: marketing/sales, product/service development/delivery, and administrative support. These major business processes and functions in general are common to every business in some form; otherwise, profitable operation would not be attainable.

To make an organization profitable, other business processes are required based on industry and solely based on the organization's unique business model. These processes are industry and core business model based. In the next chapter, we will explore these business processes and what makes them unique and central to business improvement.

Business-Improvement Model

Part 1: Business Strategy Structure

Step 1 Understand the Law of Business Reality
Organizations serve customers in a profitable way (balance quality and efficiency) or cease to exist.

Step 2 Understand the Target—The Core Business Model
Why organizations generate profit different from their competitors.

Step 3 Influencers of the Core Business Model
Pressure and Enhancers on Performance

Step 4 Embrace Business Strategy and Structure
Basis for Improvement—Whether Leaders Know It or Not

Part 2: Business Process Structure

Step 5 Common Processes and Functions of a Business Model
The Law—Inherent to Process, Functions, and Operation

CHAPTER 7

THE INDUSTRY—BASIS FOR COMMON OPERATIONAL PROCESS

It is the "birth of a new industry." I am sure that you have heard that phrase before. I was helping one of my children work on a research paper where he had to describe how the automobile started or "birthed" a new industry. I realized that a new industry is really started when an innovative product produces a nonexistent core business model to actualize. You see, when a product innovation is so influential that the innovation actualizes a nonexistent core business model, then a new industry is realized. This new industry will also cause a change in all other industries' status quo. This one product will formulate brand-new companies that will produce similar products or services within the newly formed industry. So in a sense, it is the birth of a new industry.

Innovation can change a product that is introduced into the market, but an industry will take time for a market to realize that a change has occurred. In the case of the automobile industry, many inventors of the automobile started with a carriage. In fact, the first cars were named "horseless carriages." Companies that produced carriages for horses could have introduced automobiles as a new product if they had kept up with the innovation that changed the product. But the change was not embraced by most and the carriage companies closed their doors, displaced by the change in the market for the new means of personal transportation. For improvement professionals, we must read the signs of an innovation that will change an industry and how it will affect your business and your customers.

Industry Common Operations

Industry operations are basically common business processes among each business in the same industry. If we look closer at the development of either a horse or "horseless" carriage, we notice that the production of the product was about the same operation (minus the horse or engine). Changes would need to be made to make a self-contained engine and provide propulsion rather than a horse, but these changes were the identified business improvements. The base operation for the industry remained the same and continued for the changeover to build the new horseless carriage. In fact, the way an automobile was constructed was very much the same as the carriage itself. It was not until the assembly line was integrated into the operation that the production changed significantly.

I would gather to say that the most change that needed to occur was in the minds of the carriage companies' owners themselves. The unwillingness of people to meet innovation is the first cause of lack of improvement. But that is for another discussion. For now, we will focus on the industry itself.

Like the horseless carriage industry, companies produce similar products within their industry. These common products have a set of common business processes that drive operation. These industry-based business processes are common to all companies within an industry and are a target for business improvement. Industry based business processes are the next level of business processes derived from a company's core business model. But there is more to the definition of industry-based operations and business process that affects business improvement. Let's further explore the industry and effects on business improvement.

Industry Process: Uniquely the Same

The industry a company resides in determines a number of factors that influence business improvement. Some of these factors are part of the "influencers" of the core business model and some are just common to all companies within an industry. An industry by definition is a grouping of like businesses that are in the same field of goods and services. Examples are pharmaceuticals, food service, insurance, banking, computers, airlines, clothing, and education.

A company within an industry operates similarly because customer needs being fulfilled are similar. For example, if your company operates within the financial services industry, then you are fulfilling financial needs of a customer. In turn, if you are in the food service industry, then you are meeting the needs of customer food service business. Just like all businesses have in common business operations because of the law of business reality, all industries have in common business processes within its industry for business operation.

Industry-based operations are just that—business processes that are unique to a specific industry but common to that same industry. For example, in the agriculture industry, you grow and harvest a product. There is a specific time to grow and a specific time to harvest. Each of these, growing and harvesting, has different operations and must be kept separate to preserve product quality for the customer. Can you imagine if a farmer would plant seeds in the middle of winter or harvest corn four weeks after planting? Sounds silly. But there are specific operations that are known for the industry and are unique to that industry.

In a company, there are business process that are done just because of the commonality of the company type or industry that your work in. When you work for a manufacturing company, your company needs to develop and build a product. If you work for an electric company, your company needs to generate and distribute electricity. If you work for a bank, your company needs to receive deposits and most of the time will make loans. There are just basic business processes that are performed based on the company and industry that an organization operates within and that cannot be changed.

Each industry has a set of *common* operations which are the foundation for common business process. Just like in the previous chapter about common business processes, there are common industry-based business processes. If we take a closer look at the common business processes in all businesses—marketing/sales, product/service, and administration—and then see the industry types, we can see that there are common industry-based business processes.

This is somewhat of a jump in thought for some business-improvement professionals—to think that each company within an industry has commonality yet each company is unique outside of its industry. This may seem confusing, but actually, it is the logical and normal progression from the derivation of the law of business reality to a company's uniqueness derived from its core business model. As a company further defines itself to embrace its core business model, the model will be based on its industry. Each industry has already defined itself for economies of scale, formation of resources, and people experience skill sets.

The formation of resources is a critical factor for a successful company. Without a formation of resources, a company will not be able to operate its core business model. When a group of companies has successfully maintained profitability, it will form an industry. This will define business functions, operations, and business processes that will have commonality in success. This success is leveraged by the entire industry and produces common business processes across the group of companies within their industry.

The following chart highlights the enterprise business processes that are derived by an industry and are common to that industry. Again, to service customers in a profitable way, each industry spawns successful business processes within the three main business process groups. In this way, a company will have industry operations that are common to all companies within its industry yet still have its unique business processes based on its unique core business model.

Common Industry Business Process

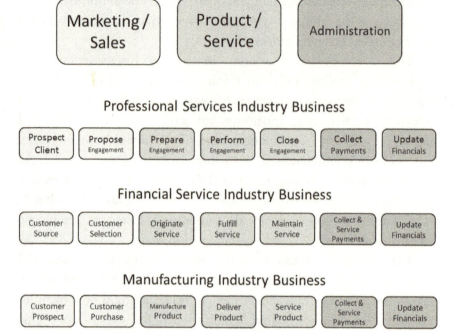

Enterprise Business Process

| Marketing / Sales | Product / Service | Administration |

Professional Services Industry Business

| Prospect Client | Propose Engagement | Prepare Engagement | Perform Engagement | Close Engagement | Collect Payments | Update Financials |

Financial Service Industry Business

| Customer Source | Customer Selection | Originate Service | Fulfill Service | Maintain Service | Collect & Service Payments | Update Financials |

Manufacturing Industry Business

| Customer Prospect | Customer Purchase | Manufacture Product | Deliver Product | Service Product | Collect & Service Payments | Update Financials |

As highlighted in the chart, each industry will derive common business processes within each of the three main process groups by definition of the law of business reality. For example, in all manufacturing companies, an organization needs to identify products, sell, manufacture, deliver, service, and financially administrate, or the company will not be profitable.

In turn, financial service companies need to source customers, select choices, originate, fulfill, maintain products, and financially administrate their company. Our last example is a professional services company. They need to perform client prospecting, propose engagements, prepare for engagement, perform the engagement, close and complete the engagement, and financially administrate the engagement. All these processes are common to each company in its specific industry, but they are unique to its industry based on the success of companies within the industry.

Best Common Industry Processes

We have discussed that each company within an industry has commonality yet is unique outside of its industry. In the consulting industry in the late 1990s, many firms made much of the term *best practices*. It was a term used to identify best business practices for a particular industry or business discipline. What it was, in fact, was best industry practices that were common across each company in an industry. This is somewhat of a misnomer. A best practice is something only each company can define for itself. An industry practice is one that is common to each industry and each company must determine if it is a best practice for its organization.

Best industry processes are derived by the company's industry. As previously highlighted, each company has industry business practices that are determined by the operating industry. Business processes are the same. The law of business reality will predetermine business processes. Like the law, the industry will also predetermine a set of common business process across an industry. So *best practices* really means "best common industry practices." An organization should really strive for the best common industry business processes as the industry has determined. Another way to state this is a common process in the industry that achieves success for the company.

An improvement professional should not get caught up in these terms. Many software and consulting organizations sell concepts before substance. Such was the case in the late 1990s. Millions of dollars were spent attempting to gain *best practices* only to fail because an organization did not understand that what was needed was to adopt best common practices and business process for their industry. These firms tried to bend themselves into operations that did not fit their organization's culture, character, and operating philosophy.

As a business-improvement professional, you are the front line of defense for your company. Sift each improvement idea to see if it fits your organization. Be cautious when reviewing so-called best practices or any idea that comes from the latest thought leaders as to the real value for improving your company. You may be the only person that has the reality of improvement and stands firm in the gap to prevent the latest really bad idea from becoming a major operational problem for your company.

I have seen an organization go into bankruptcy only because the managers and leaders of the company did not properly analyze the latest concept, innovative technology, or new method on how these so-called improvements would really fit its organization. A best practice for some companies can be a disaster for other companies. An innovative technology for some organizations could drive others into bankruptcy. Sift all new ideas and bounce them against your organization's core business model and the business process that is in operation to see if it really would improve the organization. You can then make sure you are really improving your organization.

Business-Improvement Model

Part 1: Business Strategy Structure

Step 1 Understand the Law of Business Reality
Organizations serve customers in a profitable way (balance quality and efficiency) or cease to exist.

Step 2 Understand the Target—The Core Business Model
Why organizations generate profit different from their competitors.

Step 3 Influencers of the Core Business Model
Pressure and Enhancers on Performance

Step 4 Embrace Business Strategy and Structure
Basis for Improvement—Whether Leaders Know It or Not

Part 2: Business Process Structure
Step 5 Common Processes and Functions of a Business Model
The Law—Inherent to Process, Functions, and Operation

Step 6 Industry Processes of a Business Model
Developing Industry Common Process Structure

CHAPTER 8

CORE BUSINESS PROCESSES—ENABLEMENT OF THE CORE BUSINESS MODEL

"Apples and oranges." We use this comparison all the time. When you look into the reason why we use this phrase for comparison, it is very telling. Apples and oranges are both fruit. They both have seeds and an outer skin. They both grow on trees and are used for fruit juices. Even though they seem to be almost the same, they have big differences. Apples can have different colors of edible skin like red, green, or yellow whereas oranges are just orange and usually you don't eat the skin. Apples usually are picked in the fall whereas oranges are picked in the winter. Apples and oranges seem the same but have major differences that make them very different fruits.

So it is with organizations. Even though it may seem that companies are within the same industry, their products or services will be very different to their customers. Some of these differences are based on meeting the needs of their specific customers, and some are based on other influences of the core business model. But whatever the differences between companies, the fact remains that they are different and distinct within their industry. Just like apples and oranges, companies are different or they would not be serving their customers uniquely in a profitable way.

We already know that the law of business reality is the source of common business processes. We also know a company's industry is the source of common industry-based business processes unique to its industry. Then a further definition of business process is the organization's own core business model. An organization will have specific and unique business operations based on its own unique core business model. As we have previously outlined, an organization's core business model is the reason an organization exists and maintains its viability. Since it is a derivative of the law of business reality, which is the source of business processes, then it is reasonable for an organization to enable its core business model with a set of unique businesses processes called core business processes.

Like apples and oranges, these core business processes enable a company to have its uniqueness and separate itself from other organizations for each customer. They are the differentiator for each company that is acted out each and every day in the form of executed tasks to serve customers and generate profits for their respective organizations.

For example, some organizations believe that a higher level of customer service is part of their core business model. In this case, an organization would have more emphasis on sales and service business processes than other companies in its own industry. Another example is if a company distinguishes itself based on consistency of product. Many food franchises use this aspect as part of the core business model. In this case, the franchisee would need to develop a highly consistent food preparation operation to make sure that every store would produce the same level of product quality. Each time a customer would go to a different store, the customer could expect the same level of product quality. Each company would need to have a set of business processes to enable either part or its entire core business model. These unique business processes would differentiate each company from all other companies and enable its core business model. These business processes are the core business processes of the company.

A great example in understanding the core business process differentiator is Federal Express. FedEx found that its model was not only to ship overnight but also to let the customer know where his or her package was at any point of the delivery process. This led to the company developing a customer package tracking process on its Web site. As you most likely know, any customer that ships with FedEx can find exactly where its package is at every step of the shipping process. This allows the customer to know that its package would be delivered when FedEx stated it would, thereby raising the company image. Its tagline of "absolutely, positively" was imbedded in its business process as a core business process differentiator and enabled FedEx's core business model of overnight delivery confidence (Maggiore 2012).

Everybody that I know, especially if they have children, has been to a McDonald's. McDonald's is the epitome of consistency. At any store anywhere in the United States, a Big Mac has the same taste and quality. In fact, I have been blessed to travel to China, and even in cities like Beijing, Guangzhou, Wuhan, and Changsha, in every McDonald's that I have visited, the Big Mac was the same quality and taste. Even though it took more skill to order what I was looking for (since my Mandarin is not very good), it still was a welcome site to me and my taste buds when I was in need of Americanized food.

McDonald's has built its organization on more of constancy of product, and the organization knows it. It has embraced its core business model and built strong core business processes. Each procedure is structured around product quality and consistency from store to store. Everything they have built in the supply chain to the hamburger packaging is the same. McDonald's is a great example of a company that leveraged and embraced its core business model with a set of core business processes and has effectively implemented those business processes for profitability.

Focus on Core Business Process

Many companies do not realize that core business process is the enablement of their core business model. In the many companies that I have been associated with, there are some business leaders that understand the principle of core business processes, and some that do not even understand they have a core business model.

The leaders that understand that the enablement of their core business model is enablement of their core business processes are the leaders that have companies that operate to serve their customers in a profitable way. The ones that do not understand eventually fade away without ever understanding why they could not attain profitable operations. It is a shame that so many great leaders with great ideas do not operationalize successfully, because they miss the core of a business and fail to embrace core business processes.

Whenever I start a new engagement, I start with a clear understanding of what the company does and its core business model. Then I look for the core business processes. You can tell a lot of an organization by the way they have implemented its core business model with its core business processes. All the other business process is fairly obvious, including industry-based business process. But it is the subtly of the core business model-based business processes that enable the uniqueness of the organization. Those companies that have a clear understanding and a passion to drive these processes are the companies that will perform in the upper quadrant of their market.

A great example is Apple computer in the mid-1990s. Apple computer never said that it would be the largest computer company. In fact, it had never said it was a computer company at all. Apple is the best at taking technology and making it easy and productive to use—as easy as a standard appliance. I have a colleague that worked for Apple in the 1990s who told me the vision of the company was to develop products that were as easy to use as an ordinary toaster. Apple has built its vision and business processes on enabling that core business model—as simple as using a toaster. It is still very evident to this day that Apple has successfully enabled its core business model in all its products. By not overtly focusing on profits but by embracing its core business model and core business processes, it has established itself as one of the largest and most profitable technology products company in its industry.

To be an effective improvement professional, one must find and understand the core business processes. First, understand the core business model, and then find the business processes and core business processes. Many inappropriate business processes are based on the mismatch of business process, core business processes, and an organization's core business model. If a company cannot understand what its core business process is or its business process alignment with its core business model, then it is on a line that will eventually lead it to nonprofitable operation. Based on the degree of misalignment, the company may be on a downward spiral. Most of the time, a company can read the signs and instinctively change to bring alignment back to its business processes. But sometimes, the organization does not know it is misaligned and will need help to return to profitable operation.

As business-improvement professionals, it is imperative to understand that core business processes come from an organization's core business model. It is also imperative to understand when these core business processes are not embraced and enabled, they will actually work against the company's performance. That's right. A counter action or process *friction* occurs when tasks that conform to the core business model come in conflict with business processes that are counter to the core business model. The direct effect is inefficiency; the greater effect is poor customer experience, which will lead to lost market share.

Process friction is detrimental to the organization on two fronts. First, the process is unproductive and underperforming to the company's core business model. This leads to extra work, higher costs to perform the same tasks, and lost revenue because the organization is spending more time on each task instead of attending to new tasks or customers. Second will be lower customer experience as mentioned earlier. Nothing frustrates a customer more than expectations not being met, especially when the response is counter to the main reason why the customer is pursuing the company in the first place. Think about it. A customer contacts a company based on its perceived performance only to realize that it was just that—perception and not reality. Remember it is the customer's perception of performance (the quality aspect of the law of business reality) that is important, not what you think is important. This will definitely lead to customer frustration and eventually lost market share.

A great example of not focusing on core business model business process happened to me directly while I was reviewing my insurance. For the last three years, my homeowners insurance has increased 10 to 20 percent each year. When I asked my agent why and how we can change this, she mentioned in an indirect way that I would not be able to find cheaper insurance.

Bad move, of course I perceived this as a challenge. Since my insurance company had a core business model of serving customers like we were best friends, I felt this was not what I expected from my agent. My perception was that that my agent would work hard to find a cheaper insurance for me, especially since I have been with her for twenty-three years. I found cheaper insurance, and it was 50 percent cheaper. My agent forgot the organization's core business model and her sales process did not reflect their insurance company's core business model, which resulted in a lost customer.

As you can see, not focusing on core business processes is counterproductive to overall business performance. Not executing the right business processes according to an organization's core business model will always be counter to business performance. This is a key aspect in doing the right thing for an organization in business improvement. Focus on business processes that enable the organization's core business model and you will find that your projects will be successful and doing the best improvement projects for your organization. Oh, and by the way, my old insurance company eventually reduced its prices after about two years when it realized how many customers it had lost.

Source of Enterprise Business Process

At this point, I want to make clear the cascading aspect of business process. Business process is dependent on a cascade of higher-level business process and business models. The source of business process is the operation of the law of business reality and the core business model. Let me further explain. As mentioned in the previous chapter, the law of business reality is the source of business functions, and business functions are performed by business process. We also know that an industry's common business process is also determined by the law of business reality. Plus, we have also reviewed that the core business model is the source of core business processes, which is how a company operates differently from its competitors. Core business processes come from the uniqueness of the core business model and the common processes of the business or industry. These three—the law, industry, and core business model—form the base source for all business process that executes and operates an organization. These three also are cascading in order of general operation to granular operation from the law, industry, and the core.

This cascade and the source of business process is highlighted in the following chart:

The Source and Outcome of Enterprise Business Process

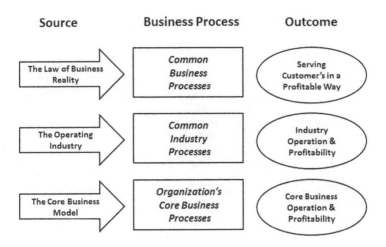

Each of these is a subset of the higher level in the business process cascade. Meaning that the core business processes are a more defined set of business processes from the industry business processes, and industry business process are a more defined set of business processes from the enterprise business process that are from the law of business reality business processes.

The law of business reality produces common business processes that all businesses will perform in some form; otherwise, the organization will not service customers in a profitable way. Each organization operates in an industry and each industry has a set of business process that is unique to its industry but common to all organizations that operate within the industry. Core business processes are unique to each organization. They enable each organization's core business model, and they enable the unique operation to fulfill meeting customers' needs in a profitable way.

Core business processes are the enabling mechanism to the core business model of the organization. It drives the uniqueness and differentiation for the company. Not focusing on these business processes can have major consequences with respect to the customer and customer expectations. Profitability depends on a productive enablement of the core business processes. In fact, profitability depends on successfully understanding the core business processes as they relate to industry-based business processes.

Enterprise Business Process

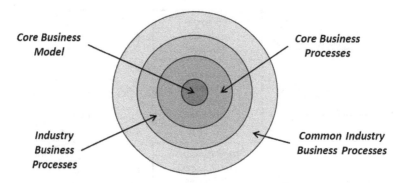

We learned that business processes are a cascade of dependency streaming from the law of business reality, the industry, and the core business model of the organization. It is the source of each level and becomes more granular in detail as we move from top to bottom and, as depicted, from inside to outside. Understanding each level and which process is required to fulfill the organization's core business process is central to improving the business holistically.

Holistically is key. Each layer separately does not fulfill the entire enterprise process and on its own and each does not complete the operations to be performed. It is the culmination of each specific layer to fill in each step accordingly to the operating core business model to where each business process gets its base source. The foundation is the operating business and the source is from the law of business reality, the next layer of business process source is from the industry to which the organization operates within, and the last is the most specific: the core business processes which get their source from the organization's core business model. All layers are present in the enterprise process, and all layers operate depend on each other. The composite of business processes from all layers working together is the composite or enterprise business process operation.

A central element to this discussion is that many improvement professionals have a difficult time separating the difference between these layers and the source of each business process type. Before an improvement professional can begin to understand which business process needs improvement, he must understand the source of each business process. In fact, before an improvement professional can distinguish profitable business processes, one must distinguish between a normal business process that has no real effect on improvement and performing business processes that do have an effect on the bottom line.

This aspect is so important and central to the organization that I cannot express the importance enough. The business-improvement professional must understand the difference between normal business process and profitable business processes; otherwise, the improvement initiative will have no impact on the bottom line or—worse—would be counter to business process improvement. The source of each business process and the identification of each type is the start of understanding performing, profitable business process.

Process Performance Cannibalization

Have you ever heard of the term *process performance cannibalization?* Process performance cannibalization happens when one part of the organization improves a process, which causes another part of the organization's business process to lose performance. That is where an improvement project did not recognize that it might cause another part of the organization to lose performance. This is where improvement projects really are counterproductive.

As improvement professionals, we need to understand when a project might affect another part of the organization and compensate for that lost performance. This usually happens when the improvement project does not follow its downstream effects in either process resources or costs. For instance, when you reduce resource allocation for an effort that is performed and adjust for service. The cost may go down, but the quality may also go down and have an adverse effect on customer behavior. This effect may reduce sales, and the end result is that the company loses profitability.

Another example may be an internal aspect. For instance, a company that I observed once determined that if it started to process most of its common paper-based forms electronically, it would pay for the project by reducing the internal transport and mail of paper. It implemented the project only to find that mail costs went up instead of down. The cause was that the salespeople were overnight mailing sales packets through FedEx. This increased the per-piece price for shipping and actually increased the cost of mailing.

When looking to improve business process, make sure you are looking at all influencers and other business processes in the organization for impact. The business process that you are trying to improve could actually be cannibalizing the very item that you are trying to improve thus causing an overall decrease in performance.

Process performance cannibalization can also be caused by process influencers. Process influencers will be explored in the next chapter and will highlight the effects outside and inside impact on process performance. For now, industry process without a doubt comprises a significant number of the total business processes performed and should be thoroughly understood to improve the business process for your organization's core business model.

Business-Improvement Model

Part 1: Business Strategy Structure

Step 1 Understand the Law of Business Reality

Organizations serve customers in a profitable way (balance quality and efficiency) or cease to exist.

Step 2 Understand the Target—The Core Business Model
Why organizations generate profit different from their competitors.

Step 3 Influencers of the Core Business Model
Pressure and Enhancers on Performance

Step 4 Embrace Business Strategy and Structure
Basis for Improvement—Whether Leaders Know It or Not

Part 2: Business Process Structure

Step 5 Common Processes and Functions of a Business Model
The Law—Inherent to Process, Functions, and Operation

Step 6 Industry Processes of a Business Model
Developing Industry Common Process Structure

Step 7 The Core Business Model Business Processes
Embrace for Uniqueness and Profitability

CHAPTER 9

INFLUENCERS ON BUSINESS PROCESSES AND STRUCTURE

There are forces that are constantly attacking your organization's process performance and structure. These forces are either outside or internal from your organization, and sometimes they're known or unknown. Sometimes, they are based in positive or negative forces to your project. Make no mistake; they are like invisible darts that can harpoon a project and cause it to spin out of control of cost or performance. These forces are known as business process influencers.

A business process influencer is any aspect that would change, alter, or modify a business process from its basic operation. Influencers in the base definition are the same as the influencers of the core business model. Since influencers can alter the core business model and the core business model is derived from the law of business reality model, then it stands to reason that the same influencers that affect a core business model will in fact affect business processes as well. Let's explore the major components as they relate to business process.

Process influencers are environmental, operation, and innovation and reflect each of the model influencers as described in previous chapters. Even though each has been described in detail of the effects on a core business model, the focus here is the type and magnitude of change and/or alteration of the business process. Since the base definition is an influencer that can actually alter or change a business process from performing its main goal, an influencer is then a performance enhancer or inhibitor that can modify a business process. See the following diagram:

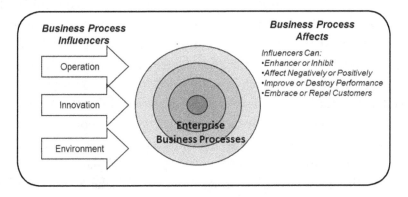

If an influencer is regulatory in nature, the regulation might cause the business process to lose performance and increase costs, customer experience issues, or higher risk aspects. If this happens, this would cause a deterioration of the business, starting with the business process, and left unchecked, ripple all the way up to the core business model. Industry regulation must be reviewed with all aspects to the influence of the performance. I have seen organizations that are in highly regulated industries get caught off guard when the regulators come out with new rules to which that they must comply without consideration for customer and profitability aspects. You will not continue to be profitable if your organization continues to react to new regulations instead of anticipating the influence of regulations on your customer experience.

What is the case if the influencer is new technology? The new technology could actually improve performance and increase profitability, which could lead to larger share in market share with improved productivity and customer service. A technology that is not vetted by an organization's core business processes can actually inhibit performance. Such the case of the innovation of the late 1990s with enterprise resource planning. ERP had great promise to improve performance, but many organizations did not compare the operating processes with their own core business processes and found their ERP projects fail or—even worse—implemented and their organization's performance did the exact opposite of what the intended technology was promised to perform. Influencers can have a positive or negative influence on the business process and process structure and must be identified and evaluated for each improvement project that is initiated.

Take for instance the environmental governmental influencer. Governments have many regulations. In the financial industry, a company must comply with a large degree of regulations. Like, in a banking organization, which is highly regulated, the regulation can be so intense on the business process that it can actually dictate the method of customer interaction. The customer does not care about the internal regulation compliance. The customer cares about meeting their needs for a loan application that has nearly fifty pages of signatures or deposit funding that requires such identity checks that make a customer feel like a criminal. These processes are far-reaching and cause a disconnect between a company and the type of relationship it is trying to establish, which is trust. If the bank in this case cannot mitigate the influence of regulation on its interaction process with the customer, then the regulation might cause a significant issue with the customer retention.

Another example is the operational influence. A large issue today is skilled resources. Based on the business model and the law of business reality, an organization must perform in a profitable way, and skilled, affordable labor costs are a significant factor in this equation. In fact, skilled resource that is cost effective is the entire value proposition for offshore, outsourced business processes. Whether it is factory assembly, mortgage underwriters, X-ray technicians, or legal court documentation processing, all parts of a business process are now examined for an outsource opportunity, and the major factor is the cost of the business operation. Plus, the entire operational question has been turned upside down because of the outsource innovation that has taken place. Not only Americans but also citizens of receiver countries like India, Indonesia, and of course, China have been affected by this operation influencer.

A third influencer is innovation. A major innovation in today's business operations is a tool called BPMS or business process management system. This software has the ability to automate business processes with the same functions, business rules, and sequence as a normal process would operate. This tool has the promise to automate tasks that normally a person would need to perform and connect the enterprise with visibility in process performance. Organizations that are successful using this innovation will be able to automate business process and provide increased performance, capacity, and most of all, increased productivity, which always leads to increased profitability. Companies that do not implement a tool could find themselves with higher pressure to perform with less-productive systems. Your business improvement is centered on innovations and the way to improve the business. The is the base requirement for business improvement, and those that embrace it will be aware of new innovations while others will watch by the sidelines and miss opportunities to provide performance for their organization.

I have seen so many business-improvement projects go down in flames because of failing to estimate the influencers of business process. Why? Because the basis of the core business process is to fulfill the core business model and make it work. If you cannot make a profitable organization, you cannot run a business. This again is a killer. So many great improvement projects fail because the operation and business process cannot be made productive enough to make a profitable organization. Failing to understand the influencers of the business process will cause every improvement project to end in a statistic.

Influencers on Process Structure

What is the real effect of the influencer to a business process? If the influencer causes a change to a business process, this could result in the change of process structure. In previous chapters, we described a process as the how and the function is what is to be performed. Influencers can alter how each process is performed and what is to be performed. Influencers can be very powerful. I have seen entire operations rendered unprofitable because the aspects of the influencers were underestimated as to their impact on the organization. As improvement professionals, we must consider each of these influencers for their impact on performance.

Since each influencer's impact can alter process structure, one must evaluate the affects from the customer's perspective and from a performance perspective including cost. If a regulation makes it more costly to produce and deliver a product or service, then the regulation negatively influences the process. If resources and skills improve the operation, then the influencer positively affects the business process. Each influencer needs to be considered for its effect on the business process and process structure for an organization.

In my experience, there are two major influencers: government regulation and innovation. Each can have effects in either business process changes or even business model modification. Government regulations can significantly change performance and interaction with customers. As well, innovation can have the same effect with performance and customer interaction. Sometimes, the innovation can trigger a government regulation. For instance, when Internet purchases became popular, many states began to lose tax revenue from the entire cross-state purchases. Since when purchases across states exempted collecting state sales tax, many purchasers reviewed online purchases as more beneficial than store purchases. The states began to lose tax revenue and made changes to their state tax laws to recoup lost revenue. This is a case where the innovation influencer affected the collection of tax revenue to which the government influencer altered the regulation in order to compensate for the tax collection. In both events, an organization altered its business process to accommodate each business process influencer.

When considering the business process structure for business-improvement projects, one must review all the influencers on business process. Not only the current and known influencers but also future influencers, as projects tend to take some time, and even years, to implement. Look at your current, past, and future process and review to see if influencers might change the way you perform business process or any aspect of the organization. Even internal politics can have an effect, and not mitigating can lead to a failed implementation or the value generated by the business-improvement initiative will not be attained.

Business-Improvement Model

Part 1: Business Strategy Structure

Step 1 Understand the Law of Business Reality
Organizations serve customers in a profitable way (balance quality and efficiency) or cease to exist.

Step 2 Understand the Target—The Core Business Model
Why organizations generate profit different from their competitors.

Step 3 Influencers of the Core Business Model
Pressure and Enhancers on Performance

Step 4 Embrace Business Strategy and Structure
Basis for Improvement—Whether Leaders Know It or Not

Part 2: Business Process Structure

Step 5 Common Processes and Functions of a Business Model
The Law—Inherent to Process, Functions, and Operation

Step 6 Industry Processes of a Business Model
Developing Industry Common Process Structure

Step 7 The Core Business Model Business Processes
Embrace for Uniqueness and Profitability

Step 8 Business Processes Influencers
Influencing Process Structure, Performance, and Profitability

CHAPTER 10

THE OBJECTIVE OF BUSINESS IMPROVEMENT

Now that we understand how process, functions, and influencers work together to form the business operation, let's talk about how we improve the business, or to be more exact, what is the real business-improvement objective? This chapter might seem a bit redundant from our previous chapter about the core business model, but this chapter connects the law of business reality, core business model, with business operations improvement. This chapter also presents examples of companies that focus on their objective and succeed or those who don't and have failed. I have mentioned before why so many improvement projects do not meet their objectives when the real issue was that the objectives were not directly tied to the organization's core business model. Here we will connect the two and further build the foundation for reality-based business improvement.

The Objective of Business Improvement

Previously, we asked why so many projects failed to produce targeted performance improvements. We answered that question: because projects did not improve the organization's core business model. Equally, we asked, "Where do business processes originate?" Equally, we answered: the realization of the core business model and law of business reality.

We now need to ask the question that seems to be lost in translation for so many business-improvements professionals: what is the real objective of business improvement?

What is the objective of business improvement?

We are asking a question that seems so obvious and seems so ridiculous that we wonder why we need to ask the question in the first place. But as improvement professionals, we need to ask this very important question. We must fully understand the objective or what needs to be improved. Without an objective, there is no specific target to aim at, no goal to attain, and no basis for improvement.

In its simplicity, the baseline of improvement is moving from a less attractive position to a more attractive position. So for business-improvement professionals, this should be the call and the cause for action. The cause is to improve to a better position. If it does not excite you to see a process, action, or business become more efficient (when a business operates better, it becomes more competitive), then you need to reflect on why you are in the business of improvement.

But improve what? To understand improvement, you must understand first what you're improving, second the objective, and third the goal you are attaining.

Improvement—the objective and the attained goal.

Since we are interested in business or an organization, we would conclude that "the what" is a business or organization. On what? Based on the fact that each business exists based on its core business model, we would conclude the "on what" should be the improvement of the core business model. To what? To what is the successful operation of its core business model? Since a business or organization's viability is based on the successful operation of an organization's core business model, then we should focus on improving the operation of an organization's core business model.

Business Improvement: Object of Improvement Identification

The What A Business or Organization

To What   A Core Business Model
On What   The Operation of the Core Business Model

Business improvement should focus on improving the operation of an organization's core business model.

True, but how is that accomplished? Since every business is based on a core business model and process is the operations or actions that are performed to fulfill an organization's core business model, as stated in a previous chapter, then we need to improve the organization's operations or business process. The object of improvement is the business processes that fulfill an organization's core business model.

The object of business improvement is business processes (operations) that fulfill an organization's core business model.

Seems simple, but in reality, it is hard for many improvement professionals to grasp this concept. Why? They miss the *connection* of the objective as it relates to the organization. Let me explain further. The main part of the objective of improvement is an organization's core business model, which is based on the law of business reality. We already know the law is to uniquely serve customers in a profitable way while balancing quality and efficiency. Since business process, based on our definition, is an organization's process and operations that fulfill or achieve the core business model, then it is the operation of a business or *business process* that must achieve an organization's ability to uniquely service customers in a profitable way, balancing quality and efficiency.

Based on that connection, process improvement is when business process is furthering an organization's ability to uniquely serve customers in a profitable way by balancing quality and efficiency. So then the objective of business improvement is to further and organization's ability to uniquely serve customers in a profitable way, balancing quality and efficiency, by using *business processes*.

Business process is directly connected to the core business model and the law of business reality. You cannot separate the two; they are so directly connected that nonperforming business process will bring down the core business model and eventually destroy the company.

> **Business process (operations) is directly connected to an organization's core business model and the law of business reality.**

That means to further a company's ability to serve customers in a profitable way is by improving business processes (and functions) based on the core business model while managing influencers on the business processes.

Remember we are trying to improve an organization, but also remember that if the organization stops either serving customers or has an inability to balance quality and efficiency for profitability, it will cease to exist by definition of the law. So when improving an organization, we cannot try to circumvent or even break the law or the core business model. It will not be circumvented or broken. A company will cease to exist before you do either one.

Business-Improvement Objective

So now we have connected the law of business reality, core business model, influencers, and business process to the objective. All four together are required for the business improvement objective. There are a few ways this connection can be stated.

One way is a change in business process that furthers an organization's ability to uniquely serve customers in a profitable way, balancing quality and efficiency. It can also be stated a little more succinctly as the objective of business improvement is change that furthers an organization's core business model. Very simple, direct, and very accurate to what an organization should focus on to improve its organization.

> **The business-improvement objective is change in business process (operations) that furthers (productively) an organization's ability to uniquely**

serve customers in a profitable way, balancing quality and efficiency.

The objective of business improvement is operational change that furthers (productively) an organization's core business model.

The objective of business improvement seems simple, but is it? A change needs to consider all the pressures of business influencers, political forces, resource changes, marketing shifts, customer intricacies, economic shifts, innovation changes, and business cycle ups and downs. This is a great task, to say the least, and a great mystery for some leaders as well. Many managers, organizational leaders, and even CEOs find this to be a revelation. For some, they find this to be instinctive, and some find this so hard to understand that they cannot articulate the concept to their peers.

Whether you understand this objective or not, it is the reality of business improvement. Some still have a hard time understanding the impacts and the effects of not embracing these simple facts. You can understand and embrace it or disregard it. It does not matter, but in the end, reality will be realized and its effects will also be realized, just like the project failure rates mentioned earlier.

Let me highlight three situations and their leadership in understanding of their organizations' core business model and its impact on organizational performance. The understanding or misunderstanding of these leaders of impact on their company was paramount to the success or failures that led to corporate viability. Let's examine three companies and their leadership.

John Scully, the CEO of Apple in 1986, still had his head in sugar water. He did not understand Apple's core business model and did not know the computer industry impact. He himself admits he was wrong for the position by his own interview.

"I came in not knowing anything about computers," he says.

"My sense is that when Steve left (in 1986, after the board rejected his bid to replace Sculley as CEO) I still didn't know very much about computers."

"My decision was first to fix the company, but I didn't know how to fix companies and to get it back to be successful again."

(Yarrow 2010)

Then John Sculley made two bad decisions. First was technical, not picking Intel for the processor, and the other was not bringing back Steve Jobs. He was unable to make decisions that could bring Apple back because he did not know Apple. John Sculley further stated his not understanding the computer industry by trying to follow Steve Jobs. He admitted, "During my era, really everything we did was following his philosophy—his design methodology. Unfortunately, I wasn't as good at it as he was" (Yarrow 2010).

John Scully could not fix the company because he did not get Apple's core business model. In fact, only Steve Jobs got it, and it is not an accident that nobody wanted to buy the company in 1993. Apple's core business model is so central to its market that it did not fit well with other businesses in its industry. It is also not an accident that the company started its growth into success when Steve Jobs returned.

The objective of business improvement is so tightly connected to the success of an industry. The following examples shows that when many companies in an industry follow the same path that is out of alignment with the industry's core business model, the entire industry can crash.

From 2009 to 2010, amidst the worst credit meltdown since the Great Depression of the 1930s, over three hundred banks failed and ceased to exist as a viable banking organization because they lost sight of their banking core business model; they wanted to serve customers that should not have had loans granted (ProblemBankList 2015). The following is the findings from the FDIC of the main causes that were consistent across all the banks that failed between 2009 and 2010:

- ineffective board and management oversight
- inadequate procedures
- volatile noncore funding

- increased loan-related losses in commercial real estate lending (Collins 2009)

You have to ask yourself what the primary operation of a bank is. A bank, by its base definition, is to provide a safe deposit for customers and to loan out capital to generate profit. The main aspect of bank management is to manage risk to reduce loss of unpaid loans. Consistent with these bank failures was the inability for these organizations to understand the basics of their industry and how it affected their core business model. Based on the stated information from these nearly three hundred bank failures, they not only missed their core business model, but they even missed the most basic of business operation for any organization, which is the law of business reality. They did not serve their customers in a profitable way, so they ceased to exist.

Alternatively, there is Mars Foods. Started like many companies from humble beginnings, on a kitchen table, Frank C. Mars learned from his mother, Alva, how to hand-dip chocolate in 1882. In 1922, he invented the Mar-O-Bar, which was renamed to the Mars Bar in 1926. In 1923 the Milky-Way Bar was introduced, then in 1930 Snickers Bar, in 1932 Three Musketeers, and in 1941 M&Ms. From that humble beginning, Frank had a firm understanding of his company's core business model while serving customers and balancing quality and efficiency. The Mars Company, still family and privately owned, began acquiring companies and, you guessed it, accurately purchased companies that match its core business model like Dove Bar. And then it moved its candies into frozen selections like ice cream-based Snickers and Three Musketeers bars (Mars, Inc. 2015).

Mars fully understood the law of business reality, and its core business model, coupled with business processes that operationalized its model, has continued to be a successful, viable, and profitable. A company that knew what were the aspects of its customers met their needs and continued to service them. This vigilant focus of its core business model, with all its distractions, including multiple wars, depressions, recessions, business cycles, endless government regulation, technology innovations, and leadership transitions, let it stay the course. But most of all, the Mars Company has been one of the longest running companies in America and, in fact, the world (Mars, Inc. 2015). This is mainly due to the leadership understanding and fulfilling the law of business reality and Mars' own unique core business model.

It is noteworthy that some boards of directors might not know the companies' core business model. They can be the chief leader and even own a company, but they might not know their own company's core business model. But the most successful business leaders know how to understand and use this information for investment.

One thing that I admire about Berkshire-Hathaway and Warren Buffet is the investor intelligence on knowing good companies to purchase. They really understand the connection between their understanding of a core business model and the operation. They understand when a company is run well. Not by the financials but by the understanding of the operationalization of a well-positioned core business model.

> Warren Buffett likes to invest in companies where management focuses on activities that are within the expertise of their company and not wander off spending shareholders' money in areas that they know little about.
>
> Keeping a company on track is obviously an attribute of sound company management and is a sound investment principle. Understanding the business so much that you know when the company can get off track.
>
> (Livy 2013)

So the next question is "Why do you think that so many improvement projects fail or underperform?" There is your answer. Many improvement projects do not focus on or even consider the organization's core business model. That is the first indicator of a failed project. Embrace this aspect. Consider this one aspect with your next project and you will avert many potential events that could cause your project to fail.

So the objective of business improvement is to change business process that furthers an organization's core business model. Period! This perspective is paramount to running a successful operation. Understand it and serve your organization to the fullest potential. Ignore it, and you will be part of the statistics that were mentioned early in the book. The best-run organizations know this aspect either intuitively or implicitly. They will express it in many different ways, but in the end, the organizations serve customers uniquely with their core business model or they will cease to exist. Focus on the objective, and you will have a line of sight that is connected to a successful project. And successful entrepreneurs and leaders know it implicitly.

With this one concept and objective, you have a better understanding on which you can operate and evaluate each project and improvement initiative. You should be able to make analysis to each value proposition and business case and ask the question "Are we doing the right thing?" for the company that is to change operations that further your organization's core business model. Now we know the objective. Another equally important question is "How do we know when the organization is performing to an organization's objective?" That is the subject of the next section and will reveal some interesting perspectives that even the best business and organizational professionals do not grasp.

Business-Improvement Model

Part 1: Business Strategy Structure

Step 1 Understand the Law of Business Reality
Organizations serve customers in a profitable way (balance quality and efficiency) or cease to exist.

Step 2 Understand the Target—The Core Business Model
Why organizations generate profit different from their competitors.

Step 3 Influencers of the Core Business Model
Pressure and Enhancers on Performance

Step 4 Embrace Business Strategy and Structure
Basis for Improvement—Whether Leaders Know It or Not

Part 2: Business Process Structure

Step 5   Common Processes and Functions of a Business Model
The Law—Inherent to Process, Functions, and Operation

Step 6   Industry Processes of a Business Model
Developing Industry Common Process Structure

Step 7   Core Business Model Processes
Embrace for Uniqueness and Profitability

Step 8   Business Processes Influencers
Influencing Process Structure, Performance, and Profitability

Step 9   The Business-Improvement Objective
Change Operations to Further an Organization's Core Business Model

CHAPTER 11

BUSINESS PROCESS AND THE OPERATIONAL PERFORMANCE GOAL

Incredibly, there is a question that seems to be at the center of many process and operations discussions, debates, and even arguments. In fact, many of my own colleagues cannot give a definitive answer to this controversial question: how do we know business processes or operations are performing? Funny that this is controversial, but it is. Sometimes, I even regret bringing up the question at the beginning of an improvement project meeting because of the heated discussion that ensues, but the question needs to be asked to make sure your project stays on target and results in true company improvement performance.

You would think with today's contemporary business-improvement environment that we would not need to ask how we know. As professionals, shouldn't we already know how our projects are improving an organization? But I believe that many organizational improvement professionals take real improvement objectives for granted. They know *what* and *when*, but they do not know *how* or *why*. Improvement professionals think they know, but they really don't, which is evident in the way they approach improvement projects.

Ask an improvement professional to give tangible evidence that a project has achieved organizational improvement. Many business-improvement professionals will give a pat answer like the following:

- When the process improvement objectives, have met with executive expectations.
- Current operational metrics are an improvement compared to past operational metrics.
- Operational costs have been reduced.

Standard stuff. But is this really evidence of performance improvement? Can they prove that the organization is better with the project it has implemented? Can they prove that the organization's core business model has been furthered or improved or has increased performance?

I have also seen where these same professionals clearly do not understand organizational performance compared to management expected goals. These improvement leaders simply lay out charts, graphs, indicators, and metrics and still do not have a clue in understanding of how the business has improved. This is why so many executives get fooled into grand enterprise programs by internal managers or outside vendors with programs that do not hit expectations and usually end up with the executives losing their positions.

In the same vein, professionals believe that technology for the sake of innovation will improve performance. This was so prevalent in the late 1990s. Many companies were sold the idea that a year 2000 project implementing a new enterprise software system (ERP) would not only make the organization compliant but would automatically improve company performance. Not only were many of these projects never successfully implemented but technology installation projects experienced budget overruns and multiple missed target dates. Companies made huge expenditures only to realize their organizations' performances were really no better off with the new system. The only improvements were a few added integrations and Web pages for customer access. These companies had poured millions of dollars into implementations just to get back to the same level of performance that they had with the previous system. Ah yes, but their organizations were year 2000 compliant.

Even worse than pouring millions of dollars into a system to get back to the same level of performance were the projects that failed completely. These projects had multiple years of litigation spending, even more capital after project-failed capital. I actually reviewed several of these failed projects as an expert witness and was able to see the utter waste firsthand. Many of these organizations took ten years to recover, and their systems took that and much more time to stabilize operations. By the time many companies stabilized after their year 2000 projects, new regulations and business cycles pushed companies to redirect project efforts, and they lost even more capital to performance opportunity. And yes, many executives continued to lose their jobs.

So what is it then for true organizational performance? Do you really understand what improvement looks like? Are you sure that reducing costs will result in long-term performance? Do metrics really point to serving your customers? Are you certain executives know how to improve their own organizations? Let's answer these questions with an exploration of organizational performance, from a core business model perspective.

Understand True Organizational Performance

So then why do so many improvement professionals not agree, understand, or even know how or why to improve their organizations?

Because true organizational performance is not so obvious and not stated correctly in current industry thought.

To gain true performance, you will need to think differently about organizational performance. How to define it, measure it, and approach improvement projects with this concept. You need to first understand improvement with the frame of the core business model with all its aspects. Let's break down the understanding of improvement that we know so far. In the previous chapter, we answered the objective of business improvement.

Business improvement is operational change that furthers an organization's core business model.

We know the focus is the core business model, but the question that seems to elude most improvement professionals is how we know that a core business model has been furthered. We know that a core business model operation is realized by its business processes. With that aspect, we now need to ask, "Is a business process performing?" That is a very different question from "Is a business process improved?"

A business process that is furthering a core business process is a performing process. Not just metrics that point to improvement (which we will discuss later in the chapter), costs that have been reduced, or meeting executives' expected objectives. A business process can be very efficient, but if it is not furthering the core business model, it is not performing. Also, no matter how effective business process performs its functions, if the process is not at a performance level that is needed by the organization, it is not a performing process. In other words, if the business process does not meet the objective that is a business process that does not further the core business model, then the business process is not performing.

If a process is furthering the core business model, the process is a performing process.

So that is it. Performance is when the operation or business process is furthering the company's core business model. So now we need to ask how we recognize a performing process. In other words, how do we detect, identify, or measure that processes or operations are furthering an organization's core business model? Detection of a performing process can be recognized in two forms: the seen and unseen. Let's first review unseen operational performance.

The unseen performance is about the holistic operation of a core business model. Meaning that when all the operations are performing, there are outcomes that are *unseen* and produce a furthering of a core business model. Unseen performance is best understood from the results and is not measured by what metrics or costs but can be seen in branding identification and customer satisfaction. The following excerpt is from the book *In Search of Excellence* by Thomas Peters and highlights this unseen performance, which is not exactly stated as a business process but is still at the heart of a core business model. Peters and Waterman note that Frito's chips and Maytag's washers should be commodities, but they own very high margins reflecting their unseen advantage.

> The problem in America is that our fascination with the tools of management obscures our apparent ignorance of art. Our tools are biased toward measurement and analysis. We can measure the costs. But with these tools alone, we can't really elaborate on the value of a turned-on Maytag or Caterpillar work force churning out quality products or a Frito-Lay salesperson going that extra mile for the ordinary customer. Worse, our tools force us into a rational bent that views askance the very sources of innovation in the excellent companies.
>
> (Peters and Waterman 1984)

Why would such commodity-oriented business make such high margins? Because of the hard to see or unseen performance that is the essence of a core business model for these companies to drive the extra performance for higher margins. We have analysis tools and cost basis, but we cannot measure a salesman going the extra mile or tools that obscure the apparent ignorance of art. In this book, we would call it the *art* part of the core business model. At the heart of every core business model is the *unseen* core value of the organization. It is the soul and unseen effect of the organization.

This *unseen* performance is sometimes equated to the company image. It is the emotional response when asked about the company. Very simply put, what do you feel about the company when someone asks you about the company name? Good, bad, great, or terrible? It is your emotional reaction to the company based on the experiences interacting directly or indirectly with the company. These emotional responses are also developed by what we call the "customer experiences" when interacting with a company. Although not part of this book, there are many articles and publications on customer experience. But for now, unseen performance is very much a part of the core business model performance and is a holistic performance measure for our perspectives.

For the purposes of this book, the *seen* performance is much easier to identify and understand. The *seen* performance is the outward interaction with customers' needs being meet on a daily basis. The *seen* performance is connected directly with the organization's core business model. The seen or identification of a core business model does not use common tools to identify performance. What needs to be understood is that a goal that connects the core business model operation and performance is the performing process goal.

Performing Process Goal

If common tools do not do an adequate job of the seen process performance measurement, then what is the way we should identify or detect the seen business performance? To detect performance, we need to know what it is we are detecting. We need to know the goal of performance, a goal that represents performance. Not just performing process incrementally better than the current operation's performance objective but an objective that represents operational change that furthers a core business model. That objective would be the business-improvement objective.

To understand this goal to meet the objective, we need to first understand the operational change and know it has produced change that furthers a core business model. Equally, we can ask the same question in a way that many improvement professionals take for granted. How do we know that there has been an operational change that furthers a core business model that represents performing business processes?

Understanding the connection of true performance is the great dilemma: understanding the performing process goal. The goal is really the question that many professionals cannot seem to agree or even articulate. Try to finish this statement: "Business processes are performing when ..." Can you definitively finish this statement? It is harder to answer than you think. When I ask the question to some of my business process improvement colleagues, I get many different responses:

- "When the process metrics have improved."

- "When the business-improvement criteria has been achieved."
- "When the process is more effective and efficient."

The problem with all these responses is there is no specific goal. Let me explain by responding to each: process metrics, business criteria, and the cross quotient of effective and efficient.

Process metrics measure a business process's outward performance, typically using cycle time, defects, dropout rates, etc. Process metrics can be developed by doing onsite measurements, line of sight, and mechanized measurements. Process metrics compare the current state to a future state for gap analysis and other measurement activities. They can even demonstrate that the future state is performing better than the current state.

Using this type of measurement, a business process is improved when the process metric indicates an improvement from the past. This is based on a simple comparison of before and after process measurements. If the process metrics have improved, then the process performance has improved. Here is the issue: an organization can see improved process metrics, but that does not directly indicate a process is at a level where the organization is profitable. It simply means that process metrics have changed but does not represent a business process is performing (i.e., performing to any goal).

Also, ask this question: "Do process metrics tie directly to improvement to the organization's core business model?" Not necessarily. Remember the *art* in the process. A process metric may not be connected to a core business model improvement explicitly. Cycle time, defects, or dropout rates may not have a core business model connection to the root cause of the activity or action. We have previously mentioned as well that performing a process faster does not correlate directly to process improvement or a performing process.

This type of metric is actually a red herring. The process metric could indicate that the future state process is improved, but if the future state does not further the organization's core business model, then the improvement has done nothing for the long-term improvement or business process performance. Plus, if there is a disconnection with the core business model, a process that is operating faster will simply make operations less performing but at a faster rate. Short-term improvements may sacrifice long-term core business model performance. A company's disconnected processes performing at a faster rate simply means nonperformance *faster*. Process metrics would be just recording the nonperformance, not actually a furtherance of the core business model.

Second is the business-improvement criterion aspect. Typically, this is highlighted or known in organizations as KPIs or key performance indicators. KPIs by definition should indicate a process, operation, or activity performance within an organization that drive to a company's overall performance. Just like the process metrics if KPIs are not derived based on the core business model, then it will drive performance against the way the company actually needs to perform for its customers.

This is a sticky situation because many businesspeople might not understand that their KPIs are defined erroneously. In fact, they might not even understand how to define KPIs that will further their organization's core business model. I would ask the question of business leaders how they know their KPIs further the mission of the company. If they have trouble answering the question, then this is where you start the conversation of KPIs. This way, you can start the conversation and lead them down the road to targeted KPIs for core model performance, without accusing them of misunderstanding or mismanagement of the company.

The third misunderstanding concept is the cross quotient of effective and efficient. Most professionals state this as simply *efficient and effective*. Let's take the efficient aspect first. Most process improvement professionals would link this back to process metrics or cycle time. Efficiency has its place, but we have already highlighted that process metrics, unless linked to the core business model, would not be an appropriate way to show performance improvement. Do not confuse metrics with performance.

So what about process effectiveness? I have a lot of objection to this term. It is, in its base definition, a nebulous term. How do you define something that is *effective*? Many improvement professional would say when it performs better. But better than what? Let's explore some common definitions.

- BusinessDictionary.com: "The degree to which objective are achieved and the extent to which targeted problems are solved."
- Merriam-Webster.com: "Producing a decided, decisive, or desired effect; an effective policy."
- Management Study Guide: "Effectiveness of a process refers to the usefulness of the process output in relation to the expectations and needs of the Customer."

All of these definitions support a concept rather than an outcome. No specific achievement is identified, just a concept to be defined "later" or based on someone's understanding of performance. The question still remains: to what end, target, or goal? Which means at best we are back to KPIs or, even worse, an emotional response based on an audience perspective that is perceived, guessed, or points to a desired response. None of these definitions points to performance that is based on a core business model. All three of these aspects—process metrics, KPIs, or improvement criteria effective and efficient—fail to directly point to a performance goal of a core business model.

Productivity and the Goal

As mentioned previously, these methods are insufficient and most are based on qualitative approaches that have been backed into a technical calculation. The reason these methods are stated this way is because these methods use a generic approach to improvement when a more distinct approach is required. Generic concepts based on generic aspects from a generic methodology will produce generic results. No specific goal is identified.

Also, these generic improvement methods have no foundation in a core business model. In fact many of the methodologies actually state that improvement is based on an executive's point of view and perceived improvement value. What happens if those executives do not have a clear understanding of their organization's core business model? Their projects are dead because the goal is based on opinion, conjecture, or a personal belief.

It is a sad state, but true of many improvement projects in our industry. A project is dead before it even begins. Why? There is no connection to the reason an organization exists in the first place or a more direct, distinct identified connection to an organization's core business model.

The base definition of improvement is when anything is changed from one condition to a more attractive condition or state. The goal of business improvement should be to make an improvement or change for the better that furthers the organization's core business model. The goal needs to be tied directly to the business, since the business is the object of improvement. That is the real goal, the goal of why an organization exists in the first place—an organization's core business model and improving operation through business process.

Then a goal must represent business process that is a performing process. As previously stated, a process that furthers the core business model is also a performing process. Since business process is the execution of functions in the organization to fulfill the core business model, then it is the operation of functions that needs to be improved. This execution is stated as the efficient operation of functional steps to further an organization's core business model. This is the goal of business improvement, changing operational functions for the *better* to further the core business model.

There is a new concept for this goal. It is *operational productivity*. Now we can represent the goal of business improvement as the efficient operation of functional steps to further an organization's core business model as productivity.

- Productivity is the efficient operation of functional steps to further an organization's core business model.
- The goal of business improvement is the productive operation of functional steps to further an organization's core business model.

Productivity based on this definition points directly at performance of an organization. Also, this is a more specific type of productivity because this type of productivity represents a core business model directly. This type of productivity is called core business model productivity.

Core business model productivity is not economic productivity. Economic productivity measures the performance between inputs and outputs. Core business model productivity measures the direct operational performance of an organization connected to its core business model. Two parts are compared and measured at the same time: the operation and the connection to the core business model. Core business model productivity is a much better goal and measurement, because it meets the objective and connects directly to the reason the company exists.

The following highlights the linkage of the law of business reality to core business model productivity:

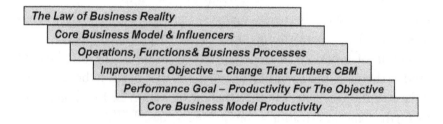

The previous diagram highlights the linkage from the law of business reality to the goal of business improvement and highlights the linkage of the objective to further the core business model to the goal of business improvement: core business model productivity. We have now connected from the law to core business productivity, which is the business improvement goal. We also know that core business model productivity is the efficient operation of functional steps to further an organization's core business model. The next question is "How do we define core business model productivity so we can measure productivity to attain the goal?" That is the topic of the next section.

Business-Improvement Model

Part 1: Business Strategy Structure

Step 1 Understand the Law of Business Reality
Organizations serve customers in a profitable way (balance quality and efficiency) or cease to exist.

Step 2 Understand the Target—The Core Business Model
Why organizations generate profit different from their competitors.

Step 3 Influencers of the Core Business Model
Pressure and Enhancers on Performance

Step 4 Embrace Business Strategy and Structure
Basis for Improvement—Whether Leaders Know It or Not

Part 2: Business Process Structure

Step 5 Common Processes and Functions of a Business Model
The Law—Inherent to Process, Functions, and Operation

Step 6 Industry Processes of a Business Model
Developing Industry Common Process Structure

Step 7 Core Business Model Processes
Embrace for Uniqueness and Profitability

Step 8 Business Processes Influencers
Influencing Process Structure, Performance, and Profitability

Step 9 The Business-Improvement Objective
Change Operations to Further an Organization's Core Business Model

Step 10 Business and Operational Performance
The Performance Goal—Core Business Model Productivity

CHAPTER 12

THE GOAL THAT IS MEASURED—CORE BUSINESS MODEL PRODUCTIVITY

You cannot have a working car without wheels. There are a lot of parts that are important to an automobile—the seats, steering wheel, and engine, for example. Yes, it is important to have an engine, but if you do not have wheels on an automobile, then it is a vehicle that you sit in and that makes lots of noise—but goes nowhere. You must have all the parts to make the car move. Lots of parts work together to do one thing—go where you want to go.

It is the same when you reference core business model productivity. When we talk about core business model productivity, we also are including total enterprise business functions and processes. Core business model productivity is the function operational performance that is connected to an organization's core business model. But when we say core business model operations, we are also including all business functions and processes: common, industry, and core business processes. We cannot have core business model productivity without the inclusion of the entire enterprise operation. It would be like an automobile without wheels. We would not be able to go where we would need to go without all the parts. The enterprise is fully connected to all other parts of the organization. We cannot have productivity or organizational value without inclusion of all business functions and processes. So when we review and analyze business processes and functions and use core business model productivity, we are also referring to enterprise-wide productivity just like the automobile.

This concept is referenced in the process strategy section, but I restate it here because so many improvement professionals think and act as if business processes are separate and compartmentalized from the rest of the enterprise. This is simply not true and is a fatal mistake. In fact, what happens in many cases is that a business process is improved at the expense of other business process performances. Performance is improved in one area of the company but decreased in another. As mentioned in the previous section, this is called *business process cannibalization*.

Business process cannibalization happens quite often and is a main reason why many projects fail to produce the expected overall enterprise improvement results. To prevent this type of improvement/dis-improvement situation, a measurement must be used that identifies and maintains enterprise improvement balance. We must be able to target areas of a company for improvement and use a consistent measurement that will compare accurately so we can ensure that positive improvement is being achieved. We must improve without sacrificing total enterprise performance. We will explore this new measurement by examining the components for the new measurement—*core business model productivity*.

Core Business Model Productivity as Organizational Value

To understand this new concept and measurement, we also need to further our understanding of organizational value. More precisely, we need to understand core business model productivity as it relates to generating organizational value. As explained in previous chapters, a process is the execution of functional goals to achieve the organization's core business model. These goals at their lowest level are functions that need to be performed and are required to achieve goals of the organization. At the same time, these functions need to be performed as efficiently as possible. So the main aspect of core business model

109

productivity is to perform the best possible functionality executed as efficiently as possible. Hence

Core Business Model Productivity = CBM Functionality : Efficiently Performed

The shortened version is

Productivity = F : E

Since the role of the organization is to produce a product or service to serve customers in a profitable way, then efficiently performed functionality that is connected to the organization's core business model generates value for the organization. If the functionality of the operation is connected to the core business model, then the performance goal, core business model productivity, will generate organizational value. To achieve core business model productivity (CBMP) is to achieve the highest level of performance an organization can achieve while this will naturally generate organizational value for the company.

Core Business Model Productivity = CBM Functionality : Efficiently Performed => Organizational Value

Shortened Version: Productivity = F : E => Organizational Value

This means organizational value is generated when core business model productivity is furthered. So when productivity increases, organizational value increases. This concept is realized when reviewing a business process. For example, when analyzing business processes as a *value chain* or a *process value* chain, one should look for core business model productivity to gain improvement and ultimately organizational value. That is where the greatest opportunity for business improvement exists.

This concept is paramount not only for the macro view of business improvement but also for business process enablement. Enablement is where the operational execution is realized. This is also the topic of the next section. For our discussions here, we will focus on the measurement, and we need to examine how functionality, efficiency, and performance are connected to drive the measurement.

Functional Goals, Efficient Execution, and the Measurement

The core business model productivity generates value from the performance of the best possible functionality executed as efficiently as possible. These functional goals along with operational business process are sometimes referred to as value streams or business process value generation. But these business processes do just that—generate value by performing what is functional executed efficiently. But we must remember not to confuse business process and functions. Business process executes functions and must perform functions for efficient operation. It is functions that are required to complete a goal and then efficient execution will generate productivity for organizational value as the outcome.

It is this combination of function and efficiency that drives performance, value, and measurement. To understand this relationship, let's explore functional components and their relation to the operation. Typically, a functional goal is the highest level of functionality that completes a specific organizational operation. But to perform the best possible functionality executed as efficiently as possible, functional groups need to be broken down into executable components. Business process cannot execute functions unless they are at a level that is executable. So a breakdown is required before a business process can execute a function. This is usually called a functional decomposition. Many times, a functional decomposition is paralleled with process decomposition. Why? because in many organizations, you will find decompositions in process form first and then functions. You will find that the sequence of functional components will follow as business process.

This can get confusing separating business process from functionality. Since most improvement projects start at reviewing the business process impacted (at least most of the successful ones do), you must ask, "What

111

is the true functional goal that is targeted for improvement?" Once the targeted functionality is identified, then you can look at the sequence of operations, which is stated as business process. Look at *what* is to be improved then look at *how* as detailed in chapter 6.

But once you have reviewed the functions, then you need to decompose the functions into components that are executable. The only way to measure performance is to break up the goals or functions into executable components. Once the function level is identified, you can review executable steps and the sequence for each function. Once decomposition is performed, you are at a level that can be identified for measurement.

Now that functionality and process are at a measurable level of decomposition, specific function and efficiency can be recognized for measurement. This is where we need to look at functionally and efficiency as different types of measurements, which we will call productivity identifiers.

Functions are measured first based on the goal that needs to be achieved and second based on the core business model. For example, to paint a car in a manufacturing process, there are several functions that are required. But the main goal is to paint the car a specific color and to the quality levels of the company. In this case, the goals would be to paint the correct color and paint adherence quality. You could say that if the car is painted, then the functional goal is achieved. But is it? If the core business model of the manufacturer is custom quality, including a multicolored, high-performance painting (let's say for NASCAR® requirements), then just painting the car is not the only functional goal. Can you imagine what the customer would think if he or she requires a custom paint job and the car comes out looking like all the others? I think obviously you would see this is not a functionally performed process and did not meet the functional goals for the expected core business model of the manufacturer.

Conversely, there is a different identifier for efficiently performed functions. Efficiency is measured first by all required steps performed in the proper sequence, second by the expected time estimates, and third based on the core business model.

Say that you wanted to get some lunch and decide to go to your favorite fast-food restaurant. You place your order and then you wait for over twenty minutes. When you get your hamburger, it is cold and missing the bun. I am sure you can see that your restaurant missed a step by not including the bun and took way too long to deliver your food. I am sure that you can also see the core business model was not furthered.

For both of these examples, functionality and efficiency can be measured. Functions are measured by the completion goals and efficiency by the sequence and duration. Both functionality and efficiency are measured and compared to the organization's core business model. Also as you can see, these components are parts of core business model productivity.

Identifiers and Components of CBMP

Functionality	Efficiency
Goals to be achieved	Steps, Time, and Sequence
Relation to CBM	Relation to CBM

Now if we use this in the model,

Core Business Model Productivity = Measurement of Performance

Measurement of
   CBM Goals or Functional Steps to be Performed
   CBM Steps, Time, and Sequence Efficiently Performed

Now we have a basis for measurement that reflects both performance and organizational value in the state of core business model productivity. Measure business process as core business model functionality performed with core business model efficiency.

When you review a business process, one of the first things you can ask yourself is if the process is based on the core business model functionality and if it is efficiently performed, including the core business model. That is the first test to see if the business process is performing. If it is not, then you have the specific components to examine to see what is not performing. Such as asking, "Is it that the functions are not meeting the goals, or are they not executed timely, in sequence, or just not meeting the core business model expectations?" With that in hand, you now have a way to understand business improvement and do the right thing for your company.

This is more a measurement of purpose than an actual hard number, but numbers can be applied. To measure by the numbers, you can identify functions as the steps to be executed to a specific goal and the process as the efficiency of the execution. Once that is set up, a simple observation of the relative expectations can produce measurements with numbers. You can take these observed measurements and apply them to a proposed solution.

Once you have a base measurement and a proposed measurement that is balanced, these can be compared and will provide constancy across the solution. This will help you level out your improvement performance and understand if the proposed solution will drive true net improvement. That is a measurement that is balanced, targeted, and based on core business model productivity.

Putting It Together—Core Business Model Productivity

Now that we have an understating of this concept, let's put it all together with an example from the banking industry. Because many people take out a loan for real estate, let's look at a simple business process for a loan origination.

To define this example, let's say there are five major business processes as highlighted in the Loan Origination Process Decomposition diagram as Level 1: Sales, Load Data Collection, Underwriting, Approval, and Close (of the application). Each of these business processes will break down or decompose further in detail. As we decompose each process, functionality is also decomposed and reviewed for each detail. Let's follow the underwriting process.

Loan Origination Process Decomposition

Underwriting is a function of risk operations and has two parts in this example. Underwriting reviews the credit worthiness of an applicant and provides a certified property valuation. In basic terms, underwriting is the analysis to determine if the applicant is a good risk to repay the loan for the property.

Underwriting decomposes into not only certain business process but also functions to fully underwrite the loan for the bank. This process will decompose into "Credit Review and Property Valuation," which is highlighted as Level 2. Part of the underwriting function is to evaluate the true value of the real estate property. Normally this is called a "real estate appraisal." In this next level, we will be at a significant level of functionality and process decomposition, which is shown in diagram as Level 3.

At its lowest level for a real estate appraisal, there are several functions that need to be completed; otherwise, the underwriting functional step is not complete. These steps might contain property inspection, comparative real estate valuations, title research, and flood review. Each one of these steps has its own set of functional steps that need to be performed to a level of completion by a predefined process. Let's look at the comparative valuations process and function.

Comparative valuations are the process of obtaining and analyzing comparable property. This is an essential process in the evaluation. Comparable property is the basis for understanding the value of a home. It is not just making a value assessment but also a market analysis, and this market analysis can be expanded to a large geographic area including construction, style, and features.

An example of functions and processes might be as follows:

Functions to Be Completed	Process Steps to Complete
Property Geography	Locate Property
Construction Quality	Validate Property
Style, Stature, Size, and Features	Compare Based on Criteria
Market Analysis	Analyze Profile
Valuation Criteria and Profile	Build Valuation Profile

Once each process and function step is identified, you can then measure the quality of each identifier. In other words, is the step functional quality of the goals achieved? You can also say if a functional step is required at all. Some governmental functions may or may not be required, so additional functions might be needed to complete the step. You can ask this easily by asking, "Is the functional step required, and is it meeting the objective?" Conversely, you can do the same question with process steps. Is the process performing the functions required as efficiently as possible?

Remember the influencer chapter? This is where it comes into play. When reviewing the functions and processes, you must always take into account influencer, such as governmental regulations being a main influencer in bank procedures. Another influencer considered is geography. Geography is a main aspect for property valuation; hence the popular phrase "Location, location, location." One must consider influencers when reviewing the process and function for productivity.

Core Business Model Productivity

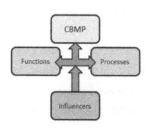

Now you can perform a comprehensive analysis. You can simply review the process step's functionality being performed as efficiently as possible. Applying a quick counting system can be implemented to give real measurements that you can compare with other processes to give you comparison improvement details.

Just as a note, if the quality of functional steps requires adding more review or acquiring extra data, then it is more than likely that productivity could be improved. This is now easily measured by counting the steps and functional goals achieved (or not achieved) for use in a comparative analysis.

Now that we have analyzed comparative analysis for core business model productivity, we can repeat for each of the process steps. Since this is a decomposition we can collapse the levels and get a cumulative CBMP measure which can be used either in detail or rolled up for comparative purposes. We then can compare, scrutinize, ask tough questions, and vet the analysis as hard as possible. That will drive a higher-level quality. This is essential. If you get it wrong here, then the enablement will fail before the project even starts.

Plan, review, and be as sure as possible. This is a very important aspect to business improvement and one where companies often miss the whole point of real improvement and doing the right thing for the company. If you are off on this point, the topic of the next section will be a disaster—*enablement* of the core business model business process.

Core Business Model Productivity—A Measurement and a Goal

One last comment about CBMP. Core business model productivity is a unique identifier for business improvement. It is not only a measurement but also a goal. So many times in improvement methodologies, we see metrics, measurements, and indicators that need to be interpreted to understand if a project or initiative has achieved its improvement goals. With CBMP, it is one in the same. No need to interpret. If productivity has increased, then by definition we have furthered the core business model and the overall goal for the company. That is why core business model productivity is so unique; it is a measurement and a goal as one.

Business-Improvement Model

Part 1: Business Strategy Structure

Step 1 Understand the Law of Business Reality
Organizations serve customers in a profitable way (balance quality and efficiency) or cease to exist.

Step 2 Understand the Target—The Core Business Model
Why organizations generate profit different from their competitors.

Step 3 Influencers of the Core Business Model
Pressure and Enhancers on Performance

Step 4 Embrace Business Strategy and Structure
Basis for Improvement—Whether Leaders Know It or Not

Part 2: Business Process Structure

Step 5 Common Processes and Functions of a Business Model
The Law—Inherent to Process, Functions, and Operation

Step 6 Industry Processes of a Business Model
Developing Industry Common Process Structure

Step 7 Core Business Model Processes
Embrace for Uniqueness and Profitability

Step 8 Business Processes Influencers
Influencing Process Structure, Performance, and Profitability

Step 9 The Business-Improvement Objective
    Change Operations to Further an Organization's Core Business
    Model

Step 10 Business and Operational Performance
    The Performance Goal—Core Business Model Productivity

Step 11 True Operational Performance Measurement
    Core Business Model Productivity

PART 2

BUSINESS OPERATION—THE BUSINESS PROCESS STRUCTURE

Section Reprise

In the last section, we discovered that business process is the operationalization of the core business model. It basically is the total enterprise process to realize your company's product or service for your customer. Business process has three major types: common, industry, and core. Each has a subsequent definition inherent to the core business model. Business processes also have influencers that are similar to the core business model influencers. Business process is equally influenced as the core business model to the actions and behavior.

Based on this business process and functions, we learned that business improvement is a change for the better and the objective for business improvement is to further a company's core business model. The best way to further the core business model is to improve the organization's functions and processes in alignment with the core business model.

We also learned that process and functions are equally important to the operations and performance. Functions are the individual goals to achieve the core business model and the process is the execution of functions. We also found out that functions and business processes operating together as the best possible functionality as the best possible execution is core business model productivity. Not only is core business model productivity the performance measurement but it also is a performance goal.

We have gone through a journey from the strategy to operational performance, and that was a lot of ground to cover. But now we have a firm base to work with, and now we fully understand how it all works together for your company. We can understand what each component is and what needs to be reviewed. We also have a way to measure from a baseline to an improved state. Not just in one area but to as small as an individual group or the entire enterprise.

Now, all we need to do is to realize the operation. That is, we need to make the operation active. This is called enablement—enablement of the business process and strategy. This is where business improvement gets interesting, because this is where the organization realizes benefits and where the customer realizes total value of your company in one great moment. The moment when they realize that you are a true and active company built to meet their needs in a profitable way.

PART 3

BUSINESS ENABLEMENT STRUCTURE

Section Introduction

In the next section, we will explore *enablement*. That is enterprise enablement using a perspective of core business model enablement. Some would say this is where the rubber meets the road. Well, it is where the operations gets realized. But the way the enterprise gets realized is really where a company can either be profitable or go bankrupt. Yes, it is that simple, yet it is the hardest and riskiest activity that the business improvement profession endeavors to perform.

Enterprise enablement is where you will be able to test out and see if a core business model is viable. This is where you will understand if your organization can operate under the pressures of influencers and meet the needs of your customer. So if that is what is meant by the rubber hits the road, well then, let's start the engines.

CHAPTER 13

BUSINESS PROCESS ENABLED WITH RESOURCES

I really like technology gadgets. I know many of my colleagues really like new technology gadgets also. When I *need* one of the latest technology gadgets, like many others, I research it, study it, and make sure it is what I want before I push the buy button. So when I have to wait, I look with anticipation for it to arrive. But then when I open the box and it is not what I expected, I am really disappointed. I think, *I did all that the research, comparison, and product configuration, and still it is wrong. And it is especially aggravating since this company had my favorite technology gadget but just could not get it right in delivery.*

Have you had a similar experience? Either the gadget was the wrong color or type or was just the wrong product completely? Then, like me, you are really let down. Not just because you received the wrong product, but now you have to go through all of the motions to try to get the right product that you had hoped you were getting in the first place. Ugh! Frustrating.

Many organizations have great ideas, products, and messages, but some organizations just can't seem to get it right. It is not a problem with the product. It is a problem with getting it done for you as the customer. If this is a common situation with a company, then the organization has what we call an enablement issue. That is enablement of business process, or it might even be more chronic—an issue with enablement of the core business model.

What Is Enablement?

A business or organization in a simple definition is a development and delivery system for a product or service. To do this simple definition, we need to fulfill or realize the organization's core business model productively. At its foundation, this is accomplished using business process and functions. The only way to realize or fulfill enterprise operations is someone or something must perform the business process. This someone or something is called a "resource." The act of a resource performing a business process is when the business process is enabled. Expanding on this concept, the ability to perform enterprise and core business model business process with resources is called the *enablement* of the enterprise operation and the core business model.

So *enablement* is the realization of enterprise operation and the core business model with resources. Remember we said that the *what* is the core business model? Well, the *how* is the enablement of business process and the core business model. Once we've decided *what* business process is required, we then need to understand *how* the business will be enabled with resources or, more directly, how the business process will be performed.

Enablement is

- the act of a resource performing a business process
- the realization of enterprise operation (business process and functions) with resources
- how business process and core business model will be performed

Business functions are just that—functions that are a list of items or goals that need to be performed. Business process is the sequence, order, and timing of functions that are performed. But how business processes get executed is by applying resources to enable each to be performed. This is where many improvement professionals have trouble. They do not see the difference among the business process, function, and enablement resources.

To highlight the differences, let's explore an example. Suppose you order food at a drive-up fast-food restaurant. One restaurant like

Wendy's® uses a person to take your order and then your order displays on a screen. You acknowledge that it is correct and the person sends it to the make line to cook your food. At another restaurant like Sonic®, you drive up to a kiosk and select your order based on the selections on the kiosk. When you complete the order, the kiosk asks you to confirm your order then it sends it to the make line to cook your food.

In these examples, both restaurants had the same order process and the same order goals were achieved, but each used a different resource to perform each process. One used a person to take the order, and the other used a kiosk. The *enablement* for the first restaurant was a person, and the *enablement* for the second restaurant was a kiosk. Even though each used a different enablement method, both achieved the food order business process. Do you see the difference? Making this distinction among business processes, functions, and enablement is central to successful business improvement.

You can have the right product, message, brand, and even target customer, but if you select the wrong enablements, it can and will impede your relationship with the customer, causing loss of capital and even completely destroying your company. I cannot express the importance of the focus of enablement and improvement project success. This is ground zero for most improvement professionals, technology leaders, and even executives. You must have a clear understanding of enablement and enablement strategy for your organization. To have a clear understanding of enablement, we must first understand enablement types.

> **Leadership must have clear understanding of enablement and enablement strategy for their organization.**

Enablement Resources

Enterprise enablement is accomplished by using resources. Resources are sometimes referred to as assets or something that provides an available means to an end. The resource is what provides the ability to get something performed or executed to completion. For business improvement, an enablement resource is the entity that performs business process and business functions to meet the core business model of the organization.

Enablement resources fall into two categories—*internal* or *external*. Internal resources are resources that are supplied by the organization. That is, the organization is responsible for performance and the business process. External resource is an enablement resource that is supplied outside the organization. External is usually when the organization has contracted with a third party or organization to perform a business process and is also responsible for the successful completion. Another name for external and a more contemporary name today is *outsourced*. Outsourced is an external resource that just means the resource outside the organization performs a business process for the organization.

An internal resource has two further breakdowns: people/animal or machine/technology. Internal resource is when the organization is responsible for the performance of the business process and it is executed either by a person or machine/technology. Like the example of the fast-food restaurant, both Wendy's and Sonic used an internal resource for the collection of order information. One used a person to interact with the customer and the other used an interactive kiosk or machine. No matter if a person or machine is used, the organization used the focus to enable the order business process to completion.

Internal Resource	External Resource
People/Animal	Third Party
or Machine/Technology	or Outsourced

Whether you use internal or external resources, each can be applied to almost any situation. You can use either resource for everything from helping to producing your product to customer service support. The type of resource references what or who is performing the execution of the business process.

Although the resource type references *who* is performing the business process, there are distinct differences in each type. Internal vs. external has pros and cons and is a major consideration for selection of which resource will be used for process enablement. Let's review each type to understand the distinctions for consideration.

Internal Resources

Internal resources specifically point to the organization supplying the ability to perform the business process. This requires either using people to perform process or some sort of machine/technology to perform the business process. In reality, it is usually a combination of people and technology. Sometimes, this is expressed as an area of focus for technology groups as a catchphrase: "People, process, and technology." This phrase needs to be put into context. It is really process, then people, and then technology. We need to focus on what needs to be performed rather than how technology will perform the process.

Since internal resources are the responsibility of the organization, the organization needs to focus on the ability to perform the targeted business process and functions. This requires an organization to build an infrastructure, including organizational structures, technology platforms, quality standards, measurements, and quality controls, to perform to the required level. With internal resources, the company has complete control over the ability for the resource to perform. It can control timing, materials—people, basically every aspect of the function, process, and resources to the performance level that is required. Not only internal resources control the level of performance, but internal resources can also control the level of enablement. Sometimes, this is called vertical integration.

Vertical integration is where the company's internal enablement resources are connected in some or all levels of the process for a product or service. The more vertical, the deeper the enablement of the enterprise process enablement including from customer selection to product development and delivery. In other words, the company enables acquisition of materials to sales of the final product. This is a large task for an organization to take on the entire production and delivery of its product or service. When looking at enablement resources and vertical integration, an organization needs to consider gains in the level of quality and investment before taking on this major process enablement.

Why are vertical integration enablement resources needed? There are four main reasons why an organization would take on such a large task as to develop all aspects of the development and deployment of a product or service. First, simple product or service development cost control. An organization that has internal development of its product or service would have direct oversight of each stage, hence the ability to control costs at each stage of the development. Second, the organization would have a need for higher quality. With higher oversight also comes quality review. An organization would be able to take advantage of the direct involvement and attain a level of quality that it requires. Third is the inability of third-party producers to develop components to specification levels required. That is, no one can develop to the cost and/or quality levels required by an organization's core business model. Fourth, and a main reason for our discussion, is to further the core business model of the organization. If an organization wants to have complete control over the impression and client experience, then the organization must control and resource the business process itself. That is the only way an organization will be able to keep its uniqueness and serve its customers in a profitable way. Vertical integration usage consideration is summarized in the following chart:

Four Points to Use Vertical Integration
1. product/service development cost control
2. product/service quality control
3. inability of third party organizations
4. further core business model control

One of the greatest and largest examples of vertical integration can be found in the early stages of the automobile industry. In 1922, the Rouge manufacturing plant near Detroit, Michigan, housed one of the largest automobile plants of all time. The Ford Motor Company built its automobiles from almost all raw materials on one end of the mile-long plant to a finished Model T that drove off the lot on the other end. You could see boats and barges on the river filled with cotton to make seats, raw glass for the windshields, coke and ore for the steel furnaces, and all the metal parts. Nearly 100,000 workers at the Rouge plant made just about every part that went into the Model T. Why?

Henry Ford wanted to control all aspects of the manufacturing process. He wanted to make sure that his Model T was the best for his customer. Ford knew since the automobile industry was in its beginning stages, there were no other suitable third parties that could build the parts to the level of quality, cost, and control that the company required. Hence, the almost complete vertical integration of resources to build Ford's automobile (The Henry Ford Museum and Village n.d.).

Fast-forward about ninety years. Tesla Motors builds an all-electric automobile. Its manufacturing plant starts with aluminum rolls that are stamped into parts to manufacture the body of its Model-S. But instead of using humans to assemble the Model-S as in Ford's manufacturing plant, Tesla uses over one hundred and sixty robots while controlling quality and costs in its process (*Wired* 2013). Vertical integration of resources is the method that Tesla used to maintain its goal of producing a high-end electric automobile.

Recently, to further control costs for Tesla's ambitious mass production, it decided to target the single highest cost in its product—the battery pack. Tesla plans to build a large factory to produce battery packs to reduce the manufacturing costs while increasing capacity quality. Called the Gigafactory, Tesla plans to build a plant that can reduce the manufacturing of battery packs by 30 percent, making Tesla able to produce an electric automobile for the mass market (Tesla Motors 2014). With Tesla's Gigafactory added to its existing manufacturing process, Tesla will further use vertical integrated manufacturing resources in its production, which already has a significant process efficiency control and cost-reduction effect.

External Resources

Just like internal resources specifically point to an organization supplying the ability to perform business process, external resources point the ability to perform the business processes *outside* organization.

In other words, a third party will perform all of the business process to the level of quality and cost level that is expected by the requesting organization.

When a primary organization contracts an external resource, the responsibility for business process performance shifts to the contracted or thirty-party organization. It is then the organization's responsibility to understand how to set up designs and product specifications for the thirty party to drive the expected quality. But the main responsibility for the organization is to monitor product quality and vendor production performance. The organization will need to build a purchasing department that has very tight vendor management procedures to make sure that the outside firm is delivering to expected quality and the contracted price point; otherwise, the parent company will not be able to fulfill its core business model.

Since the organization has delegated the operation, it is the responsibility of the thirty party to perform the business process or produce the necessary product or service requested. This requires the thirty party to understand specifically the organization's core business model and build an infrastructure, technology platforms, quality standards, measurements, and quality controls to perform to the required level. With external resources, the company has delegated complete control to the thirty party to perform. It needs to control timing, materials, and people—basically every aspect of the function, process, and resources—to the performance level that is required. Now the organization needs to manage only one aspect—the thirty party's performance.

An organization can view the third party as both a pro and a con. The third party that has a stake in how other organizations perform the same business process or produces the same products or services should be able to reduce costs based on economies of scale. This is also a situation where other organizations basically have the same product or service as your organization and would give you no differentiator to your competitors. Using third parties that have horizontal integration, meaning leveraging other companies for the same product service, must be used with great understanding. That is understanding that this is not where your organization's core business model is furthered. Horizontal integration most of the time is to support a basic operation that most likely is an industry based operation. It is used for a business process, product, or service that is common to the entire industry. There is no core business model benefit.

A great example of horizontal integration is in the personal computer industry. The CPU of a computer is used in every unit that is produced. A major and dominant producer of CPU chips is Intel®. Intel grew to large size when personal computers using the Windows operating system leveraged its CPU chips in the late 1980s and 1990s. Many computer manufacturers started their business based on the Intel CPU chip set. The competitive industry grew so fast that the personal computer became a commodity yet Intel keep its dominance. Intel, using marketing catchphrases like "Intel Inside" and direct marketing to consumers helped to push manufacturers to use its chips. The marketing paid off as Intel became a leader in computer units while most Windows-based operating system computers used an Intel CPU. Where others struggled to gain traction in the highly commoditize market, Intel remained at the center, growing and producing more chips for significant market share. Intel was successful using horizontal integration for other manufacturers while maintaining its dominance in the personal computer industry.

Dell Computer was among those in the industry and was square in the middle of the personal computer market. But Dell Computer knew that the Intel chip was not a differentiator. In fact, Dell built its company on its core business model by supplying customer-configurable personal computers in a very efficient process. Dell provided a way for each customer to select different components and have a unit built to customer specific needs. Dell built an assembly line that could assemble efficiently different units. Thereby, Dell was able to provide and serve customers uniquely. Dell did not fall into a trap like others and understood that the CPU was not a differentiator. Because Dell knew exactly what its core business model was, it became a large player in the highly competitive personal computer industry while using horizontal integration for the Intel CPU chip correctly.

133

Internal Resources—People

When you think of an enablement resource, sometimes we do not think of people. We assume that the business process will just get done. But in actuality, people are the number one business process enablement. Think about it. People are needed for customer service call centers, product development and design, transportation, and many other processes required for enterprise operations. Unless your organization can be fully automated or fully outsourced, you need to look to people to get business process performed and completed.

But many companies do not consider that to be true. In fact, some companies see the human resource department as a sunk cost rather than as an asset. The basic truth is that the performance of people will be the largest increase of productivity for your company, if the appropriate levels of skilled, trained, and tasked people are according to your core business model. Can you imagine if 10 percent of your company's human resources were trained and skilled on erroneous information? That would cause complete mismatch for your company and send productivity into the abyss. People enablement is a major factor in core business model enablement and must be considered a major part of the total enablement architecture.

Internal Resources—People—The Organizational Structure

Since the first enablement to be considered is human resources, then the first structure that should be reviewed is your organizational structure. You can find a lot out about an organization by its organizational structure chart. Why? Because where the people are focused is where the company focus is going to be. People need direction, and if the structure of the company is not focused on productive aspects of the company, then the enablement will suffer and not fulfill the core business model.

Look at your structure. Is it focused on what the company is all about? Does it look like it is enabling the core business model directly? If not, that is a good place to start with business improvement.

Gather information about the business process and see if there is a misalignment with the organizational structure that supports the business process. There is where you can find waste and quick wins in business improvement. As a business-improvement professional, you should always look at the organizational structure, especially when reviewing your enablement architecture.

Also, if there is restructure, realignment, or business transformation that needs to take place, the organizational structure will be the place to start and will cause the most culture impact and change in an organization. So do not take it lightly or for granted. I have seen projects stop before the project charter ink has dried just because the business improvement leader assigned did not consider the impact to the project sponsor's own restructure that would have been impacted by the proposed project.

Internal Resources—People—The Culture

One other factor to consider is the impact of culture. With people, there is always an inherent culture in an organization. Culture is a major factor in productivity and change management. When you study an organization's human resource structure, include a review of the culture. If an improvement initiative includes major changes in operations, then the culture of the company will be a factor. You cannot change it, force it, or will it, to transform, unless the culture allows it. I have seen full leadership structures collapse because they could not succeed in changing the *will* of the organization to change with them.

There are only two ways to change culture: change the minds of people or change the people. You can only change the minds of people if the people want to change. That is, they have to been given a reason, a convincing reason, to modify their behavior. If the people do not want to change, then you will see a very pervasive condition of passive aggressive behavior. This behavior occurs when personnel act like they are changing, but really they are allowing your initiative to fail—not try to change at all. As mentioned in the introduction of the book, I have seen this behavior bring down many projects. The organization and leadership must be able to convince the people to change their minds, thereby changing their motivation to the new operation.

The second way to change culture is change the people. Yes, you might need to change out or displace the current staff and/or leadership to gain the required culture change. I have seen many different methods for this change, not all of which I would endorse. One example is to move departments to different locations and leave the existing staff behind. Another method is to outsource the departments and then rehire the existing staff you want to keep to new positions. Restructuring the department is another method to gaining the resources that will promote the require culture.

There are many different aspects for the human resources to be considered—skills, talent, ability, education, etc.—but here we will focus on the ability for human resource to enable a business process. For an enablement structure, we need to understand the relationship between performance and the ability for the human resource to perform a business process. That is what you should focus on when considering a person or some other resource should perform a specific business process. That is in consideration to further the core business model in a productive manner.

An enablement structure needs to understand the relationship between performance and the ability for human resource to perform a business process.

Also, I did not miss the fact that in this section I would also talk about animals. In fact, I did consider calling this the "organic" internal resource section for all "life" resources. But I felt that the days of using horses and cattle are not relevant, so I stuck with people only.

Internal Resources—Technology/Machine

Technology (and Machine) automation is not only the number one influencer, but also technology has changed the world and has affected business improvement profoundly. The growth of technology over the past century is astounding and we have seen momentous changes in our society. Think about it, automobiles, personal computers, personalized smart phones, and of course, the Internet. Technology is so much an influencer in the industry that we have a catchphrase called "disruptive technology" for major innovation can alter the current direction of an entire industry.

Technology and ensuing innovation is such an impact on business improvement that I will devote an entire chapter on this influencer. The basic issue with technology at this point is to understand that it is part of the total organization's enterprise enablement and enablement architecture. Technology is not a be-all-end-all to enablement. I really caution you at this point to not get so wrapped up in technology's apparent ability to change a business. You can easily get sucked into this trap. What you need is fully understand the real impact of technology on an organization.

Yes, technology offers great opportunities for automation and potential productivity, but I have seen where businesses have automated one area of their company and then lost productivity in another. The way an organization would compensate for lost productivity is the company would hire more people to complete the process. That would add more cost to the entire process and would lose all the added benefit from the technology initiative. The solution must be evaluated for how the technology will be used to drive performance. That way, the appropriate level is applied for the best possible productive enablement. Although there is significant effort to make a fully automated business process with no human interaction, there still will be a need for business process supported by people to complete the business operation.

Hybrid Resource Enablement

Hybrid resource enablement is a mix of enablement between internal and external resources. Hybrid enablement, more specifically, is where a company believes that business process is best enabled by using a combination of internal and external resource blend. An example in customer service explains this situation.

An organization might find itself with high volume of customer service calls. Since the company has identified most of the customer service calls are simple and quick answers, the company decided to use an offshore customer call center to receive calls and answer the majority of quick answers. For the more complicated calls, the first line of customer service personnel documents the questions and then forwards them to an internal, more specialized, group that can answer the complicated inquiries with more depth. In this way, the company is able to accommodate increasing volume with a mix of external resources that manage less complicated calls and leverage internal, higher-skilled personnel for complicated calls. This hybrid resource enablement allows the organization to reduce overall resource costs to the organization.

Enablement and Resources Recap

Business process enablement is the act of a resource performing a business process. There are two types of resources: internal and external. Internal resources are the responsibility of the organization for producing performance. External resources are external or third party resources responsible for performance and the organization is responsible for selecting and monitoring the third party's ability to perform.

Different resource types have pros and cons to their ability to enable productive operations. Whether it is human resource or technology, each must have the ability for performance; otherwise, costs will increase. Enablement architecture must consider many of these aspects to develop a structure that will further the organization's core business model. Now we will explore how we can use core business model productivity as a directive to build an architecture that furthers the organization's core business model and operations. It is said that business process enablement is where the rubber hits the road for business improvement—true. But now let's understand what is under the hood.

Business-Improvement Model

Part 1: Business Strategy Structure

Step 1 Understand the Law of Business Reality
Organizations serve customers in a profitable way (balance quality and efficiency) or cease to exist.

Step 2 Understand the Target—The Core Business Model
Why organizations generate profit different from their competitors.

Step 3 Influencers of the Core Business Model
Pressure and Enhancers on Performance

Step 4 Embrace Business Strategy and Structure
Basis for Improvement—Whether Leaders Know It or Not

Part 2: Business Process Structure

Step 5 Common Processes and Functions of a Business Model
The Law—Inherent to Process, Functions, and Operation

Step 6 Industry Processes of a Business Model
Developing Industry Common Process Structure

Step 7 Core Business Model Processes
Embrace for Uniqueness and Profitability

Step 8 Business Processes Influencers
Influencing Process Structure, Performance, and Profitability

Step 9 The Business-Improvement Objective
Change Operations to Further an Organization's Core Business Model

David A. Duryea

Step 10 Business and Operational Performance
The Performance Goal—Core Business Model Productivity

Step 11 True Operational Performance Measurement
Measure the Goal: Core Business Model Productivity

Part 3: Business Enablement Structure

Step 12 Business Process Enablement
Resources to Realize the Core Business Model

CHAPTER 14

TECHNOLOGY ENABLEMENT OF BUSINESS PROCESS

Technology professionals sometimes have a hard time with me. Not that I try to be a problem for them. In fact, I go out of my way to get along with them and help them in every way possible. I have a lot of information technology implementation experience and understand technology's value, but sometimes they still have a hard time with me. Why? Because *it's not about technology*. It *is* about the business, organization, and serving customers first and always. Sometimes, technology professionals forget this principle.

Don't get me wrong. Technology is great and promises great automation, transformation, and organizational cost reduction. But it is not about the technology itself. The focus of technology should be on the enablement. That is, the *appropriate* technology enablement. This is not about how great technology is or how technology will change your company. It is about how to further your company's core business model. The ability for any technology enablement is to do just that—further an organization's core business model. Otherwise, the technology could disrupt operations, increase costs, and even cause your company to dissolve.

We can never lose sight of what technology enablement really is and what it means for your organization. Enable the business productivity and profitably and you will have a-best-in-class technology group. You will also be among the best technology executives in your industry.

To achieve this level, first you need to understand the real impact of technology for your organization. Not only how to use technology appropriately but the appropriate levels for your organization. Let us keep technology in perspective and make sure that we consider the real impact for your organization. To help keep technology in perspective, let us review some reality-oriented points about technology and enablement.

Technology Cost

Technology is *very* expensive. In many organizations, the technology or the IT organization is among the single largest administrative budget in the company. This is especially the case in the services and information technology industry, where these departments are considerable size as a percentage of total revenue. In a Gartner report for 2014, some of these costs are up to 7 percent of revenue of the organization (McGittigan and Solanki 2013). Companies' spending on information technology continues to increase, and the percentage of usage continues to take large chunks of capital. We have also seen where ERP (Enterprise Resource Planning) project budgets have consumed 15 to 20 percent of revenue to gain very little return, especially if the project is canceled or fails completely. Technology budgets are very large and must be managed closely to the company's core business model goal to return the invested benefit.

As companies continue to depend on technology to help drive costs reduction and increase productivity, organizations continue to grow their IT departments. This increase also creates the need for leadership to focus on management of the department. The IT department faces an every growing complexity of tools, systems, clouds, and generally more outside services to assist in IT management. As companies grow, IT demand grows and IT support grows, which increases IT budgets just to support the growing levels of IT infrastructure. Technology spending tends to be almost self-perpetuating. With this growth, the weight to manage IT departments become self-absorbed and causes slow-moving reactions to market trends and business requirements. This will make it difficult to next to impossible to react to business demands and in-turn a direct impact on business-improvement projects.

In addition, we have previously mentioned the failure rates of information and technology projects. With 60 percent to 85 percent IT project failure rates and with over $200 billion in wasted projects a year, one must be very careful to make sure everything has been done to make sure your projects are successful (The Standish Group 1994). Not just from a completion aspect but also from fulfilling the objective and more directly, further your organization's core business model. Capital is a one time and on one project expenditure. If the expenditure effort does not further your core business model, then the project is sure to fail to meet your organization's overall goal. Technology is very expensive. Know your business improvement project objectives before you start will meet or further your core business model, or the project might be dead from the beginning.

Some technology projects are so expensive that failure will force the company into dissolution. During the close of the previous century, year 2000 projects' were just that, so expensive that it actually drove companies into dissolution. We mentioned AmeriServe and its ERP project in chapter 5. The cost of its implementation compared to the return for the implemented technology was very high. During the planning stage, the high cost was not considered when the company designed the enablement structure. Due to the high costs and the inability for the ERP to perform, the ensuing losses and lack of performance prevented the organization from maintaining a viable operation, and eventually AmeriServe went into bankruptcy.

When planning an enablement strategy, one must consider all costs involved with technology—not just the initial implementation costs but also the cost to maintain, support, and enhance the entire technology enablement structure. The purchase price is only a small fraction of the total cost of ownership with technology. The total technology cost ownership is where many organizations miss technology investment analysis. One must understand the total cost of enablement to design and structure a total real benefit for the organization. Real benefit must be understood if your core business model will benefit with the proposed technology enablement. A miss-calculation will cause a company high capital losses including the possibility of organizational dissolution.

Technology Complexity

Technology is very complex. Many business professionals do not understand the complexity of technology in their organization. To set up, maintain, and impact your organization with technology requires a significant effort and a very skilled IT leadership to manage their structure. In addition, technology requires understanding of an entirely different skill set that might not be common to the organization. Even organizations in the technology industry will have a different skill set for business improvement than the technologists developing your product or service. Hard to imagine an organization that does not use at least the basics of technology, but even the basics require skills that many business professional might not possess. Make sure you take into consideration technology complexity and the skills required to manage a complex performing IT organization.

Also, with larger organizations, the technology complexity grows. Each company will need to own its technology so it can best serve its organization. Technology ownership requires having many highly skilled individuals and an operational structure for the organization. A typical technology organization would include a group that understands the enterprise operational structure. This group, to maintain performance for the company, usually will have enterprise architecture. The enterprise architecture group would map out and understand each component and how it fits into the larger operation and technology management. These operations are complex structures that require a significant amount of focus and resource, evidenced by many organizations now having a general enterprise architecture organization.

In a performance-driven technology organization, enterprise architecture will contain large numbers of components to manage. These large number of components will require the understanding of interconnects and dependencies across the organization. Each of these components has a specific purpose and understanding. Without understanding their specific purpose, interconnection to the organization is impossible and in-turn the ability to connect to and further the core business model is impossible.

Technology enablement gets even more complex when trying to understand the direct application enablement and the interaction of intersecting applications across the enterprise. Think about it. For every process that an organization performs, there are many, even tens of hundreds, of lower level sub-processes that need to be performed. For each of these sublevel business processes, for technology to enable, they must have as many applications to perform them. This enormous amount of applications is required and requires management to maintain performance.

This is reality; complexity for many organizations is the norm. For example, a simple transaction has cross interactions required to operate a single sale's transaction. But it is not simple when it comes to using technology. The main reason for the complexity is technology is non-intelligent. It is only as intuitive as the person who designed and developed the application. Technology is designed for a specific purpose and requires a lot of strategic thinking to make the application fulfill its intended business functionality. All possible combinations are considered when developing a process; otherwise, productivity will be lost. This increased development and interconnection by definition will add more complexity as the technology tries to meet all organizational functions.

When approaching a business-improvement project, understand that technology enablement is complex. It will require scrutiny and understanding, because the technology must be inclusive of the entire business process. Not just a basic process or industry best practice but the business process that is your core business model. It will require leadership to understand the true impact so that you can fully understand the impact on your core business model and in-turn the success of your improvement initiative.

Technology Requires Precision

Technology requires precision, meaning technology needs a certain level of specificity to develop applications accurately. Previously, we said that technology has a specific purpose and requires a lot of strategic thinking to make sure that it is designed to fulfill business functionality. True, and many times, this level of specificity is best implemented in a custom-developed application.

But custom development is very expensive. Many organizations, to reduce costs, have purchased ERP (enterprise resource planning) systems that claim to have functionality and business processes for best-in-class specific operation. The trouble is that most of these ERP systems at best have only industry-based business process and functionality. No ERP system will have your core business model's specific business process and functionality out of the box. This level of precision with any predefined application is at odds with the core business model uniqueness. It just is too expensive for vendors to have your core business model precoded into their application. So every ERP implementation will require at a minimum detailed configuration, if not customization. Sometimes, this requires outside developed applications as add-on to the ERP to make sure the core business model's uniqueness is preserved.

If the core business model is not addressed, then an improvement project or ERP implementation will suffer in time, cost, or the resulting operational performance from the purposed solution. It is an axiom, no matter what you plan, to strategize or account general applications will not produce specific results. Many times, the entire operation will make a significant adjustment or fail completely. You cannot have both. You must accommodate core business model business process and functionality either the project will go over budget with iterative adjustments or fail completely.

Such was the case for Agrobiotech, as I learned from testifying about its situation as an expert witness. Agrobiotech was a company that produced and grew grass seed for retailers such as The Scott's Company. The company was a small operation until mergers and acquisitions consultants suggested the company make acquisition of smaller companies to grow its organization. The issue was that each company ran its organization very differently from Agrobiotech. With each acquisition, the company simply tried to add sales and receivables to its current administrative systems. This method became problematic since each of the new companies had very different operations.

To fix this operational issue, the M&A organization suggested implementing an ERP system. It said Agrobiotech could implement the best practices in the application and move all the operations to the new application. But there was a big problem. Each company's operation did not quite fit into the application best practice. So then the consultants suggested changing each merged company's business processes to the ERPs industry's best practice process in the ERP. Big mistake. The operation did not change and—worse—the project did not implement. In fact, the organization had such operational problems that eventually the company went into bankruptcy and ceased viable operation.

The project had two issues. First, they did not understand the acquired core business model was very different and the effect this would have on the business process. Second, they believed that the ERP would be able to merge operations regardless of individual core business models. Remember the core business model generates profits, so it will resist any change to core business model process. If it is a contest between the core business model and the technology, the core business model will win every time over a technology implementation. When you approach an improvement project, understand that technology is precise and difficult to make major modifications, especially if it involves a core business model process.

Do not be fooled. No vendor can have your core business model out of the box, and no merged company is exactly the same in reference to technology. Review and understand exactly how a technology was designed so you can fill in the gaps to make sure that your business-improvement project will hit the proposed requirements and performance.

Application technology is designed to a specific philosophy and function. You cannot change philosophy easily. There is power with a well-designed application technology and great power in specifically designed technology, but general designed technology will result in general implementations. So if your company has a very specific core business model, then it is very likely that a general out-of-the box solution will not work for your organization. You must use technology for the precision based on its original design; otherwise, you will go into the seemly endless iteration of rework that has caused many of improvement projects to fail.

Technology Is Not a Core Business Model

Technology is not a core business model. More specific technology cannot fix a broken core business model or replace the need for a core business model, although technology marketing would make you think it is possible. How many times have you seen the marketing hype of new technology? The marketing is incredible for the introduction of new products. You have most likely seen it too—much hype but not much help.

The reality is technology cannot fix a broken or bad core business model. I have seen organizations pour large amounts of capital into a transformation project that had no hope of being successful. Why? Because the core business model was broken, nonexistent, or not viable. An organization must first prove out that its core business model is sustainable before new technology is applied. It is true that many new companies are developed with technology, but the core business model must be sustainable regardless of the enabled technology for stable, continued operations. Completely busted models are dead companies and cannot be fixed with any amount of new technology. Test the technology by looking first at the core business model then at the enabling technology to see if the organization is viable. Once you cut through it, you will find the real value to see if it in reality will further your core business model. Remember technology cannot fix a dead model.

Another great example of a broken core business model came from another experience as an expert witness with Nexteriaone, a communications company that was put together from a merger of three smaller organizations. The brainchild of an investment banker and M&A organization, Nexteriaone was to provide communication services for a region that was underdeveloped. Two problems with the formation of this organization were that there was no specific understanding how this organization was going serve its customers uniquely and the CIO was the former analyst hired internally from the M&A organization. Not understanding how to run either a significant information technology group or how to run the company's technology projects.

The newly formed company decided to implement a popular ERP to join its separate operations. The problem was there was no direction on how to implement. Why? No core business model. They started down one path and when they could not implement, they tried to switch ERP systems in the middle of implementation. Problem was no budget for the switch, and they were caught in multiple implementation iterations. This caused many budget overruns and then litigation when vendors were not being paid. The company continued and limped along with very little return that the M&A company was hoping it would gain. Eventually, the company was sold without ever attaining the proposed performance. Like many other companies with great ideas but no foundation of a core business model, Nexteriaone was split into little parts and sold off, having never been a significant player.

Technology Needs to Further the Core Business Model Performance

I am passionate about what technology and innovation can do for an organization. I will be one of the first to review and consider technology. The trick is truly to understand how it will help your company. Not just the next shinny object that comes along but actually how it will further your organization's core business model.

Improvement products that claim they will give your organization a *quantum shift* in improvement are usually wrong. Technology cannot fix a broken core business model. Make sure the technology you are analyzing can perform, but also make sure that you understand your core business model before you review a recommended technology. Otherwise, you will get a deer-in-the-headlights effect from the marketing bombardment and invest in technology that might not help and even hurt your organization in the long run.

If we use the objective and goal of business improvement as our basis for enablement analysis, then the definition would be to productively and profitably enable a business process that furthers an organization's core business model. That should be the focus. Understanding the objective to further your organization's core business model is the key to understanding technology performance. Implementations fail on this specific point and in turn fail in performance.

A great example of technology enablement that furthers a core business model is found in Domino's Pizza's all-in-one system. Being in a highly competitive market, Domino's knew that efficiency is the key for its franchisees' success and is a major aspect of their core business model. They built custom software specifically for its stores that would be able to take orders and run the "make line" as efficiently as possible. This system was so effective that it actually could predict future orders based on patterns within each store, thereby reducing product waste and increasing profits. When the system first was introduced, it was a bit expensive; in the long run, it has proven to be a significant reason why Domino's was on top in its industry for that time.

Technology Innovation and New Products

Technology and the influencer of technology are not only about the operation of the company. Technology innovation is also about how a main product was originally developed. In fact, most new business models start with some sort of innovation and a new product introduction. For example, the rise of the dot.com companies was due to the harnessing of the Internet. Now common names like Amazon, Ebay and Netflix are due to the innovation of the internet, and of course the social media industry was born from this introduction.

Other companies used innovation to start, such as Steris, which first used liquid sterilization for medical devices when the industry used heat (Steris n.d.). Jayco RV's used the crank for its lift systems in the pop trailer camper. Correct Craft innovations used the center outboard I/O engine for its Ski Nautique boats. Sony developed the first commercially successful transistor radio, called the Sony TR-55. The financial industry has been transformed with the Internet with all-online services like Ally Bank and Esurance. Innovation and technology have not only changed existing business models and transformed operations but technology has started new companies with products born from innovation.

Technology Enablement Recap

Organizations must understand exactly what technology will do for their company. Technology can enable a company with great potential for productivity, profitability, and customer experience innovation. But organizations need to understand that not all technology is designed to meet their specific core business model requirements. Each technology project needs to be analyzed specifically to understand the real performance that will be attained. You as an improvement professional need to be cognitive that technology is expensive, complex, and requires precision. It is not a fix for a broken core business model. The main aspect for technology enablement is that it must further your core business model productively and profitably. If you implement technology that furthers your core business model, then your organization will excel to higher levels of productivity and profitability and serve your customer in ways that no other competitor will be able to do in your industry.

Business-Improvement Model

Part 1: Business Strategy Structure

Step 1 Understand the Law of Business Reality
Organizations serve customers in a profitable way (balance quality and efficiency) or cease to exist.

Step 2 Understand the Target—The Core Business Model
Why organizations generate profit different from their competitors.

Step 3 Influencers of the Core Business Model
Pressure and Enhancers on Performance

Step 4 Embrace Business Strategy and Structure
Basis for Improvement—Whether Leaders Know It or Not

Part 2: Business Process Structure

Step 5 Common Processes and Functions of a Business Model
The Law—Inherent to Process, Functions, and Operation

Step 6 Industry Processes of a Business Model
Developing Industry Common Process Structure

Step 7 Core Business Model Processes
Embrace for Uniqueness and Profitability

Step 8 Business Processes Influencers
Influencing Process Structure, Performance, and Profitability

Step 9 The Business-Improvement Objective
Change Operations to Further an Organization's Core Business
Model

Step 10 Business and Operational Performance
The Performance Goal—Core Business Model Productivity

Step 11 True Operational Performance Measurement
Measure the Goal: Core Business Model Productivity

Part 3: Business Enablement Structure

Step 12 Business Process Enablement
Resources to Realize the Core Business Model

Step 13 Technology Enablement—Consider the Real Impact
Technology Must Further the Core Business Model

CHAPTER 15

BUSINESS PROCESS ENABLEMENT— RESOURCE APPLICATION

Have you ever been involved in a software, technology, or vendor selection process? If you have, you know that these assignments can be both enlightening and difficult. To do these selections requires you to take quite a bit of time out of your day. But the most difficult part is that it so hard to judge one vendor or product from another. Many times, each vendor does not have exactly what your company is looking for or does not meet your project requirements. So you then have to take a highly educated guess. Not the best way, but it is the only way for you to complete the analysis. Moreover, you still wonder, *Is this really the best choice?*

I know I have been in situations like that. I tried so hard to make sure that we were selecting the best vendor for the company, but there just was not an exact way to perform the comparison between all the vendors. The reason this happened was we did not have a great way to make a specific comparable analysis for our selection.

This happens all the time. When reviewing or engaged in a vendor selection, we come up with the best possible evaluation criteria, but when it comes down to making the final decision, we either guess or there is a preconceived winner already chosen. Since the scorecards are subjective, it comes down to an opinion. Why? We do not have a

David A. Duryea

common way to do an evaluation based on the company's core business model.

If we want to do the right thing for the organization, we need to look at this process in a different way. We need to look at it from a fulfillment of the core business model perspective. Selecting enablement resources and/or third-party vendors is a critical decision. When selecting a vendor or an enablement product, we need to understand that we will be engaging in a relationship. Yes, a relationship that requires our company to trust in the vendor's application to perform as part of our own organization. So we need to make sure that this is the right decision for the company. We need to make that important decision, as it will affect the company for the long term. Picking the best resource enablement is at the heart of business improvement. So let's explore the best way to select and apply enablement resources.

Applied Enablement Resources

When we review a vendor or run a product selection process, we are really looking to apply a resource to enable a particular part of company operation. But what does it really mean to *apply* a resource. Enablement means that the resource will perform the process. So that means we need to select and *apply* resources to *activate* a business process so the process will *operate* or *execute*. Sometimes, we say that we implement systems which are really applying resources to activate or perform a business process. So making application is activating a resource so that it can enable a business process to perform or operate. Basically, resource application is implementing a resource so it can perform the business process. As improvement professions, we need to take special interest in the application (implementing) and enablement of a resource.

The total enablement of a resource is the activity that helps us understand where the best resource is selected for the organization. To best perform this activity, we need to study and understand all aspects of the company. Then we need to apply resources to enable business process to perform operations to fulfill the organization's core business model. This is a critical part of business improvement, because applying

154

resources for enablement is where the organization realizes the full operation of the company.

Applying resources for enablement is where the organization realizes the full operation of the company

Selecting application resources for enablement can be tricky. We need to make sure that we analyze a resource based on two criteria. First, we need to analyze the resource for application ability. Not all resources, regardless of how great they sound or how they perform for other organizations, might be a good fit for your company. Reasons could be culture, operations capability, maturity, and a number of other reasons why a vendor's product is not implementable for your company. The second reason is the ability to perform the business process. That is the ability to meet the objective: perform business process to further the organization's core business model.

Resource Enablement Selection Criteria
1. **Resource Application** *Ability*
2. **Resource Enablement of CBM** *Ability*

Enablement is the successful implementation and execution of resources to perform a business process. For successful enablement, resources must have the ability to perform a business process within a company's structure. We need to look at the resource and ask, "Can and will a resource be able to perform a business process based on the core business model (including any influencers)?"

How do we know that a resource can and will perform a business process per the objective? When we look at applied resources, we are really looking at the business processes that will be enabled. Resource enablement needs to fulfill the goal of the objective for business improvement. From our previous chapter, we know the business-improvement objective is operational change that furthers (productively) an organization's core business model. We also know that CBMP meets the objective with a way to measure the actual productivity generation

155

as it meets the objective. Using the productivity aspect, we now have an understanding and a goal of business-improvement enablement. That is, business improvement is the enablement of business process that productively and profitably furthers an organization's core business model. We also know that CBM productivity is connected to a resource's ability to enable a business process to meet the objective.

We now have a complete understanding of resource enablement. It is applying resources to enable productivity and profitable business process that furthers the core business model. It is this definition that will be the key to improvement projects and vendor or product selections, including major improvement decisions.

> **Business-Improvement Enablement: applying resources to enable business process that productively and profitably furthers an organization's core business model.**

Business-improvement enablement meets the business-improvement objective. When business-improvement enablement connects business process that furthers an organization's core business model, your company will be successful and will reach the highest goal with resource enablement. Think about it. Why do an improvement project? Why select a product or vendor in the first place? Understand this basic concept. If you cannot improve productively or profitably, why change? And if you cannot further the core business model, why do it at all? If you can improve productively and profitably *plus* further the core business model, you have improved the business in the best way for the organization.

> **If you cannot improve productively or profitably, why change? And if you cannot further the core business model, why do it at all? If you can do both, then you have improved the business in the best way possible for the organization.**

Productivity Generation

Productivity generation is how we determine the best resource enablement and will complete the enablement selection criteria. We previously mentioned that CBM productivity is connected to a resource's ability to enable a business process to meet the improvement objective. This productivity connection is also required for analyzing resources for enablement. We know that core business model productivity (CBMP) is a business model process that is functional, efficient, and described as

Core Business Model Productivity = CBM Functionality: Efficiently Performed

Shortened Version   Productivity = F : E

For core business model productivity (CBMP) to be impactful, we need to understand a particular usage of a resource. You see, the way a resource is applied and implemented would give an indication of business process enablement quality. This enablement quality will result in core business model productivity generation or simply productivity generation.

So when a resource is enabled by a business process, productivity generation will be produced. This productivity generation results in two elements: the *amount* and the *level* of quality enablement. We can use this level and amount to compare the enablement quality for each resource and give us a real way to compare resource enablement utilization.

With productivity generation, we can now compare each resource's enablement productivity. Very simply, we can say if the resource productivity generation is greater than another resource, then the resource with the higher generation would be a better-proposed resource selection. As an example, we would propose selection by the highest return described as follows:

If CBMP (Resource 1) generation is greater than CBMP (resource 2) generation, then select resource 1.

This would indicate that resource 1 would give an organization a higher total CBM productivity than resource 2. With this productivity generation comparison, an organization will get a clear understanding of resource evaluation. In fact, when I have used this method, many vendors are somewhat perplexed by their score and have had a hard time explaining their low generation for the organization.

Productivity generation comparisons help improvement projects determine which vendor, product, or software system would **really** be the most productive for the organization. It is direct and pragmatic and gives clear understanding as to which resource will perform the best for your organization.

But to complete this analysis, to select the best enablement resource, there is one more component that needs to be considered. That is the cost or total investment for each resource. When we compare resource investments with productivity generation, we will know which resource is the best enablement resource for the organization.

Resource Investment Cost

Resource cost is interesting. As we explored in the previous chapter, people are a main enabler for organizations, and even though very flexible, human resource can be very expensive with a lack of economies of scale. Also, technology is another main enablement resource for many organizations. But technology with a large capital infrastructure investment is very expensive and sometimes prohibitive for some organizations.

Third-party resource enablement at first seems easy and less expensive, but when we consider the total cost of owning the value generation, it is not much less expensive. With all enablement resources investment/return is a significant analysis point. Cost for a resource is the balancing aspect and a major determination factor for resource enablement.

To do an accurate and complete resource evaluation, we need to consider the investment cost of the applied resource. As referenced, there are two cost aspects for an applied resource: cost of application and cost of enablement. The cost of application can be equated to the implementation of each resource. This includes the total acquisition, transition, and organizational modification (change) cost for the resource. Resource maintenance costs are all the costs for the identified period of time and cost to maintain the resource.

Resource Application Cost
- total implementation cost (acquisition, transition, organization change)

Resource Maintenance Cost
- total maintenance costs for an identified period of time

Total Resource Investment Costs = Application Costs + Maintenance Costs

Once we have identified the total investment cost for each resource, we need to evaluate each resource with its associated cost. I think it is obvious that each resource's associated cost varies among resources. But the key is to determine which resource for the amount of investment is the better resource for the company. The real evaluation is using the total investment cost with the productivity generation factor to determine the best enablement resource. This would be referred to as the best-invested productivity generation resource for the company.

Best-Invested Productivity Generation

Very simply and directly, the best invested productivity resource is the resource that has the highest productivity generation with the most reasonable resource investment. Notice I did not say the *least cost*. As many business improvement, technology, and process professionals already know, sometimes the least cost is not always the best. Other factors should be considered. These factors include resource stability, economic environment, company fit outside of the functional considerations, or company character. But most of all, the resources need to further the core business model and fit into existing organizational structure.

To complete the resource enablement understanding, we need to relate productivity generation with the resource's investment. The best way is using a ratio between the productivity generation and resource investment. With that, we can state one of the following:

- **Productivity Generation/Resource Investment**

- **CBM Functionality : Efficiently Performed**

  Total Resource Investment

- **F : E**

  I

This would tell us that a specific amount of productivity generation is produced by a resource investment. It will also tell us that we will get a certain level of functionality performed efficiently for our total investment of a specific resource. With this, we can now use it in our previous example to complete the evaluation.

> **If (resource 1) generation/investment is greater than (resource 2) generation/investment, then select resource 1.**

We now can say that resource 1 will be more productive for the total investment for the organization than resource 2. Now you can see that a business process that is enabled with a resource investment that generates productivity that furthers the core business model will be the best resource enablement.

It is still up to the improvement professional to determine the other factors that may influence specific organizational impact, but at least there is a common way to compare resources for their real impact. That is, impact that is the best-invested productivity of any vendor, product, software, or technology enablement. And then this will, in reality, improve the business the right way, including process and technology enablement.

Keep in mind that this is not just a single resource enablement but a holistic improvement perspective. The productive and profitable enablement concept can be used at multiple levels. From the lowest procedure level to enterprise value chains, you can look at a group or one high-level process. Whichever. It does not matter. Productivity generation is holistic and can be used at whatever level makes the most sense for resource evaluation and enterprise evaluation.

You can apply the productivity/profitability over the resource investment cost to gain the correct level for comparison purposes. This is key and allows for strategy evaluations at one level, and then dive into details for execution scoping. The goal is the same at any level. With it is a powerful comparison for developing project benefits at whatever level that you need to compare to make the right decision for your organization. The productivity/resource cost or the best-invested productivity is the key perspective to build an enablement operation that will drive true organizational performance.

Chapter Conclusion

Now that we have understanding of the best resource for enablement, we can make decisions for the organization with confidence. We can now determine resources and select with a consistent measure that will find the best resource for the organization. Plus, we will not only make the company more profitable but also provide the best performance for the customer. We have one last item to review to complete business improvement and do the right thing for the company. That is building an enablement structure for the organization that is designed for productivity and profitability.

Business-Improvement Model

Part 1: Business Strategy Structure

Step 1 Understand the Law of Business
Organizations serve customers in a profitable way (balance quality and efficiency) or cease to exist.

Step 2 Understand the Target—The Core Business Model
Why organizations generate profit different from their competitors.

Step 3 Influencers of the Core Business Model
Pressure and Enhancers on Performance

Step 4 Embrace Business Strategy and Structure
Basis for Improvement—Whether Leaders Know It or Not

Part 2: Business Process Structure

Step 5 Common Processes and Functions of a Business Model
The Law—Inherent to Process, Functions, and Operation

Step 6 Industry Processes of a Business Model
Developing Industry Common Process Structure

Step 7 Core Business Model Processes
Embrace for Uniqueness and Profitability

Step 8 Business Processes Influencers
Influencing Process Structure, Performance, and Profitability

Step 9 The Business-Improvement Objective
Change Operations to Further an Organization's Core Business Model

Step 10 Business and Operational Performance
The Performance Goal—Core Business Model Productivity

Step 11 True Operational Performance Measurement
Measure the Goal: Core Business Model Productivity

Part 3: Business Enablement Structure

Step 12 Business Process Enablement
Resources to Realize the Core Business Model

Step 13 Technology Enablement—Consider the Real Impact
Technology Must Further the Core Business Model

Step 14 Enablement Resources Application
The Best-Invested Productivity (CBMP)

CHAPTER 16

CORE BUSINESS MODEL ENABLEMENT— REALIZING CBM

Have you ever interacted with a company and then said, "Wow! That company has its act together"? You just know that every time you communicate with that company, things just seem right on target. And if there is something that is not exactly correct, its employees will go out of their way to make it right. You have the confidence that the company has your best interests in mind and, most of all, really wants you as a customer. Well, that situation is evidence of an organization that has a strong culture that is built on a strong core business model, including a mature enablement structure.

Enablement Structure

As mentioned before, we can make all the plans we want and all the strategies, but if we cannot enable the organization's core business model, that is *serve the customer uniquely in a profitable way,* the company will not succeed. Business processes and functions of the core business model need to be fulfilling productivity and profitability for the organization to be successful. Organizations must fulfill this first and most basic goal to be successful. To fulfill this goal, an organization must design and deploy an enterprise-wide operational business enablement also known simply as the enablement structure.

Business-improvement enablement, stated in the previous chapter, is applying resources to enablement business process that productively and profitably further an organization's core business model. An *enablement structure* is then the application and deployment of enablement resources to service customers uniquely in a profitable way (fulfilling the core business model). Simply put, the total of all enablement resources across the enterprise is the organization's enterprise enablement structure.

> **Enablement structure is the application and deployment of all enablement resources across the enterprise to service customers uniquely in a profitable way.**

An organization's operation will use many different resources to fulfill its core business model. Resources are not just thrown together; they are integrated so that business processes and functions are synchronized to fulfill the organization's operations. These operations, when working together with an organization's culture, will produce the out-front service to the customer. When the operation is working the best, it is serving the customer the best.

But that level of performance does not come easy. In fact, many organizations spend years and countless iterations trying to attain that level of customer service performance. I have seen organizations struggle just to figure out how to integrate a few simple applications. When these companies get down to the reality of their implementations, they think they are doing the right thing; but in the end, all they did was implement a few applications with loose integrations that enabled an anemic customer service. These loose integrations actually caused more iterations and more damage to the total customer experience including pulling down enterprise productivity.

One such example is an anonymous not-for-profit organization that decided to implement a popular enterprise resource planning system to help organize its sponsored funding. The organization centered on providing grants for colleges and universities to further specialized education and capital projects. When the organization selected its ERP, it did not inquire about the ability to perform fund accounting integrated to its donated grants. The organization had to build a special application just to import these transactions. The development for the application was a significant portion of the total spend for the ERP and in the end caused more transaction issues and reduced the productivity benefit for implementing the ERP in the first place. The organization did not see that the poor integration caused the entire application not to produce the necessary performance to operate per their core business model.

Another case in point to a misuse of enablement resources was in an organization that builds trailers for a dealer distribution model. This unnamed organization tried to use a third-party transportation organization to deliver its trailers to its dealers. At first, this seems like a great idea because the organization would not have to incur the overhead. But this company, as part of its core business model, was to make sure that the right trailer floor plan was sent to its dealers in a timely manner. This way, the dealers had the available product for their customers in a timely manner. But when the trailer company had trouble integrating its systems to provide the delivery organization with proper delivery information, it found out that deliveries were delayed by the third-party delivery company. Not only were its trailers delayed, but it also found out that the third-party delivery organization had contracted with its competitors. The trailer company found out very quickly that this was totally counter to its operation and its core business model; hence, it lost sales just because it did not want to manage its deliveries to its own dealers.

Like this not-for-profit and trailer company found out, selecting and integrating resources are a key consideration for building an organization's enablement structure. In fact, the two most important factors in building an enterprise enablement structure are the integration between resources and the best-invested productivity across the enterprise. Let's look at each of these factors to see how they will impact selection and performance of the organization.

Resource Integration

Resource integration is a key factor for selecting resources. Not one resource will be able to enable the entire organization's operation. So it is imperative that an enablement structure takes into consideration the ability for resources to connect with another resource. This is a significant task since, most of the time, resources will not be able to integrate without some modification. Think about it. Most resources are from third-party vendors, and many are competitors. It is the responsibility of the organization to build their integration across the enterprise.

This is where many companies fall flat. They assume, take for granted, or—even worse—believe a third-party vendor that says its product or service will integrate with other software/hardware products. Big mistake. I have seen many implementations just stop because of the failure to connect simple transactions between sales and production or not being able to provide product-costing information to the financial systems. If you have been part of a failed project, I'll bet you could see this situation happen. The organization just could not seem to get an operation running correctly, and for the customer service system, this type of misintegration spells disaster for the front line for your customer.

When selecting an enablement resource, make sure of the effort to integrate into the existing enablement structure. It will require effort and sometimes major modifications. Be sure of the real effort and cost that is required to integrate a resource. It may take some tests and even conceptual mockups. Make sure you get answers to these two questions: will the resource integrate to fulfill your core business model *and* what are the real costs to get a resource to integrate to the required level of performance? Take this into consideration for your enablement resource, and you will prevent a lot of rework and even prevent a project failure.

Enterprise Best-Invested Productivity

The other important factor in building an enterprise enablement structure is the best-invested productivity across the enterprise. The best-invested productivity generation for a resource will give you the best choice for enablement. For the enterprise, we need to understand the total best-invested productivity for the organization's operation. Think about it. If you want the best operation, then you want the most productivity for the least amount of investment. The summation of best-invested productivity for all the enabled resources will be the most productivity for the least investment. As demonstrated in the following chart of an on-line retailer business.

On-Line Retailer Business

$$\frac{FxE}{I}$$

Total Best
Invested Productivity

$$\frac{FxE}{I}$$

Group Best
Invested Productivity

$$\frac{FxE}{I} \qquad \frac{FxE}{I} \qquad \frac{FxE}{I}$$

Individual Best Invested
Productivity

When looking at the previous chart, we can see the total productivity for each resource defined as functionality multiplied by efficiency over the total investment for each enabled resources. If the resource that enables "Ship Package" can be replaced by another resource that will generate a higher level of productivity or lower the enablement costs, then we should consider the other resource for a replacement. But do not forget about the implementation and the integration of the new resources. If we consider the total impact—and it is a greater impact ((FxE)/I)—then we as improvement professionals should consider replacing the current enablement structure with the new resource.

The ***enterprise enablement structure*** is a picture of the total enabled enterprise operations. Meaning, in total how the organization is enabled to operate. The enablement structure is a significant part of the total performance of the organization. Building the enablement structure is the process of selecting and implementing resources to enable the core business model. This design is the understanding of how the company is organized and how the company will perform.

> **Enterprise enablement structure is the picture of the total resource enablement for an organization and how it will operate.**

When a business-improvement professional looks at an organization's operation to improve, it is not a simple exercise. There are so many aspects to consider that it can be difficult to manage. In fact, many executives, managers, and leaders will have disagreements and even battles of control for which resource would be selected. When developing or modifying your enablement structure, you must have a plan. Otherwise, you will be misguided by the many influencers that face your core business model. To do the best for your company, you must have a plan to select and implement resources based on your company and your core business model strategy. It is your enablement strategy.

Enablement Strategy

Well, we are almost to the conclusion of business improvement and close to the finish line. We have one final step to help your organization do the right thing. The last step in this journey is to build your organization's enablement strategy.

Enablement strategy is the approach to design and build the operational enablement structure that will realize the core business model for the organization. It is essentially the approach that you will use to build your organization's enablement structure. Companies need to make sure they have a sound enablement strategy so they can cost-effectively build an enablement structure. This is required not only to fulfill the organization's core business model but also to realize the vision of your organization's profitable operation.

> **Enablement strategy is the approach to design and build an operational enablement structure that will realize the core business model.**

You see, an enablement strategy is all about putting a puzzle together. Every piece will fit correctly in its right place. When the puzzle is complete, then you will see the total of all pieces in a complete picture. The real issue is what that picture looks like and what pieces are required so the picture does not change from its original view or vision.

Executives want a certain picture, business leaders want a certain picture, influencers will push to a certain picture, and even employees will push for a certain picture. Also, the resources that you select to design and build your enablement structure will shape the picture including vendors. All of these factors will shape, bend, push, and pull the enablement structure to a final form. You need to make very certain that you as the business-improvement leader know what is the target state picture and how it will realize the core business model. This is the hardest and riskiest activity that the business-improvement professional will perform.

Enterprise enablement strategy is where you will be able to test out and see if a core business model is viable, if a resource can actually operate or if your personnel can serve your customers. This is where you will understand if your organization can operate under the pressures of influencers and your third parties will meet the expectations of your clients. This is also where you can make or break the entire operation and be an industry leader or the next bankruptcy. So we need to cross the finish line strong, and we need to develop a sound enterprise enablement strategy.

Most of the time, an organization will have a current enablement structure. So you will need to study it to see what the current enablement strategy was when building the operation. But when you do modify your enablement structure or analyzing a new project for implementation, developing a sound and functional enablement strategy is crucial. I found that this is a very critical part in attaining your organization's core business model, so I wanted to highlight some steps to help understand the process to build or modify an enablement structure for your organization. This is the most rewarding process as a business-improvement leader, because it is enablement of the organization to do the right thing for your customer.

Main Driver

The first step to understanding how to build a sound enablement strategy is to understand the main driver or *why* are we making a change. Change drivers can come from many different sources and influencers. Not all drivers are good or valid. You need to evaluate the reason the company wants to make the change and question whether it is a valid reason. Will it improve operations and further the organization's core business model? There are so many pressures to change that a single driver needs scrutiny to understand if the reasons are valid to move forward.

Understand the Impact

Once a change driver is valid to move forward, the next step is to understand the impact of the change. Every change has an impact to an organization; the real issue is to analyze all impacts, not just from the immediate area but also to the total enterprise. In many cases, a change in one department can have enterprise implications. When developing the impact case, make sure that you understand the major components of the business improvement, including process, functions, integration, and resources. Lay out an initial enablement structure before and after, so you can identify the impact areas (with all components). This will also help you get the full picture of the impact and thereby make reality-based decisions. This is a critical step regarding why many projects fail, because they underestimated the total impact to the organization.

Cost Considerations

Once an initial enablement structure with impact considerations is developed, a reality-based cost structure needs to be built. So many times, a true costing is hard to develop, especially when trying to include integration costs and costs of all iterations for implementation. My advice is to continue with the enablement structure before and after and identify the costs with all identifiable iterations. Then if resource vendors are involved, identify the integration costs for each major vendor change. That is where costs may be overlooked. Also, just because it is the same vendor with the integration point, it does not mean there is a clean integration. Vendors are constantly merging with other companies and might not have a clear integration path. All integration and iterations must be considered, or total enablement costs will be inaccurately defined.

Execution Ability

Along with costing, execution ability is crucial to understanding enablement strategy and the performance for each resource. To be very direct, a resource's ability to perform is the bottom line. This includes your own organization's ability to perform. To build an enablement strategy, you must know—and I mean *know*—exactly your resources and your organization's ability to execute. You cannot assume when building an enablement strategy and you cannot guess when deciding on a project. Think about it. It does not matter how good a resource is if your organization does not have the capability to implement or integrate with the resource. When considering your enablement strategy, understanding execution and the ability to perform will make or break your total enablement and operation. Pay very close attention. You might be the only one that is considering the ability for a resource to execute for a business-improvement initiative. This consideration will help save your company from a very big mistake. Get the right execution, and your company will be among the best in its industry.

Now you have the components to build a sound core business model based enablement strategy. It is now a matter of just doing it. The process of developing a sound enablement strategy is in great part the most important part for a business to operate productively and profitably. The design is a great part of doing the right thing for your company and serving your customer in the best way possible.

The car is built. The engines are running. Let's run the race to win.

Business-Improvement Model

Part 1: Business Strategy Structure

Step 1 Understand the Law of Business Reality
Organizations serve customers in a profitable way (balance quality and efficiency) or cease to exist.

Step 2 Understand the Target—The Core Business Model
Why organizations generate profit different from their competitors.

Step 3 Influencers of the Core Business Model
Pressure and Enhancers on Performance

Step 4 Embrace Business Strategy and Structure
Basis for Improvement—Whether Leaders Know It or Not

Part 2: Business Process Structure

Step 5 Common Processes and Functions of a Business Model
The Law—Inherent to Process, Functions, and Operation

Step 6 Industry Processes of a Business Model
Developing Industry Common Process Structure

Step 7 Core Business Model Processes
Embrace for Uniqueness and Profitability

Step 8 Business Processes Influencers
Influencing Process Structure, Performance, and Profitability

Step 9 The Business-Improvement Objective
Change Operations to Further an Organization's Core Business Model

Step 10 Business and Operational Performance
The Performance Goal—Core Business Model Productivity

Step 11 True Operational Performance Measurement
Measure the Goal: Core Business Model Productivity

Part 2: Business Enablement Structure

Step 12 Business Process Enablement
Resources to Realize the Core Business Model

Step 13 Technology Enablement—Consider the Real Impact
Technology Must Further the Core Business Model

Step 14 Enablement Resources Application
The Best-Invested Productivity (CBMP)

Step 15 Design Core Business Model Enablement
Attain a Productive and Profitable Organization

RECAP—SUMMARY

*N*ow *you understand* how crucial it is to have a good understanding from the law of business reality to your organization's own core business model to a sound, functional, and cost-effective enterprise enablement strategy. It is cascading relationship that starts with the essence of the organization to the enablement of resource for performance-based operation.

Now you can see the direct relationship and how it affects not only your business but every business. It is the reality-based improvement that so many organizations seem to try ignore or circumvent. Now you have insight to the misguided leadership's styles, failed enablement initiatives, and disintegrated operation models that have led to failed projects and bankrupt companies. But in turn, you now have the methods to correctly drive your company to be one of the industry leaders.

The business-improvement stack is an easy way to see and understand the steps of the reality based business-improvement structure. It shows each step as the gray shades show the connection with each major group: strategy, process, measurement, and enablement.

The Business-Improvement Stack

Now it is up to you. You can use these principles to build successful, reality-based improvement for your organization. Anyone can say they can improve your company, but how many really know your core business model and what is best for your organization? You now have what you need to help fulfill objectives and serve your customer in the best way possible. You know how and have a structure to engage business improvement, so you can do the right thing for your company, including the business process and the technology resources that work best for your company.

Now let's go and be the best.

WORKS CITED

Business Dictionary. http://www.businessdictionary.com/definition/business-process.html (accessed February 17, 2015).

BusinessDictionary.com. http://www.businessdictionary.com/definition/effectiveness.html#ixzz3S6nzlaDG (accessed February 20, 2015).

Business Insider 2012. Business.Insider.com. August 21, 2012, http://www.businessinsider.com/marissa-mayer-wants-to-give-every-yahoo-employee-an-iphone-2012-8 (accessed August 15, 2016)

Business Insider 2016. Business.Insider.com. January 6, 2016, http://www.businessinsider.com/yahoo-is-prepping-to-lay-off-10-percent-or-more-of-its-workforce-2016-1 (accessed August 15, 2016)

Cantara, Michele, Samantha Searle, Anthony J. Bradley, and Bruce Robertson. "Three Best Practices Can Prevent Big Change from Destroying Your Business Transformation Initiative." *Gartner.* November 26, 2014. https://www.gartner.com/doc/2926418/best-practices-prevent-big-change (accessed August 2014).

Cars.com. http://blogs.cars.com/kickingtires/2010/01/toyota-recalls-23-million-vehicles-over-sticking-accelerator-pedal.html (accessed February 17, 2015).

Collins, Michael E. *Federal Reserve Bank of Philadelphia*. 2009. http://www.philadelphiafed.org/bank-resources/publications/src-insights/2009/fourth-quarter/q4si2_09.cfm (accessed February 20, 2015).

CNBC 2016. www.cnbc.com. May 12, 2016 http://www.cnbc.com/2016/05/12/ex-employee-claims-wireless-charging-start-up-ubeam-is-a-sham.html (accessed September 12, 2016)

Forbes 2016. www.Forbes.com. http://www.forbes.com /sites/briansolomon/2016/07/25/yahoo-sells-to-verizon-for-5-billion-marissa-mayer/#4298c2971b4d. (accessed September 12, 2016)

Gartner. *Gartner.* July 2, 2013. http://www.gartner.com/newsroom/id/2537815 (accessed August 2014).

Horovitz, Bruce. *USA Today.* December 16, 2009. http://usatoday30.usatoday.com/money/industries/food/2009-12-16-dominos16_ST_N.htm (accessed February 17, 2015).

Ivy Business Journal. May /June 2009. http://iveybusinessjournal.com/topics/strategy/how-general-motors-lost-its-focus-and-its-way#. VNlNCtLF98E (accessed February 17, 2015).

Livy, Julian. BuffetSecrets.com. January 21, 2013. http://www.buffettsecrets.com/sticking-to-what-you-know.htm (accessed February 20, 2015).

Maggiore, Dick. innismaggiore.com. October 22, 2012. http://www.innismaggiore.com/positionistview/read.aspx?id=104 (accessed February 20, 2015).

Management Study Guide. http://www.managementstudyguide.com/process-effectiveness-measurement.htm (accessed February 20, 2015).

Mars, Inc. Mars.com. 2015. http://www.mars.com/global/about-mars/history.aspx (accessed February 20, 2015).

McGittigan, Jim, and Sanil Solanki. *Gartner Report G00247911.* Gartner, 2013.

Merriam-Webster.com. http://www.merriam-webster.com/dictionary/ effective (accessed February 20, 2015).

On Site Sources at McConnell's Mill.

PapaJohns.com. http://papajohns.com (accessed February 17, 2015).

Peters, Thomas J., and Robert H. Waterman. *In Search of Excellence.* Warner, 1984.

ProblemBankList. problembanklist.com. February 3, 2015. http:// problembanklist.com/failed-bank-list/ (accessed February 20, 2015).

Rouse, Margaret. *TechTarget.* http://searchcio.techtarget.com/definition/ business-process-management (accessed February 17, 2015).

Steris. "History and Timeline." Steris.com. http://www.steris.com/ media/PDF/history/Web-History-Timeline-Dec-13.pdf (accessed February 20, 2015).

Tech Crunch. Techcrunch.com. May 11, 2016 https://www.techcrunch. com /2016/05/11/charged/ (accessed September 30, 2016).

Tesla Motors. TeslaMotors.com. February 26, 2014. http://www. teslamotors.com/blog/gigafactory (accessed February 20, 2015).

The Chicago Tribune. March 4, 2012. http://articles.chicagotribune. com/2012-03-14/opinion/ct-edit-andersen-20120314_1_andersen-s-professional-standards-group-andersen-case-founder-arthur-andersen (accessed February 17, 2015).

The Henry Ford Museum and Village. http://www.thehenryford.org/ rouge/historyofrouge.aspx (accessed August 2014).

The Standish Group. "The Chaos Manifesto." 2010.

The Standish Group. *The Chaos Report.* The Standish Group. 1994.

Wikipedia. http://en.wikipedia.org/wiki/Business_process (accessed February 17, 2015).

Wikipedia. http://en.wikipedia.org/wiki/History_of_General_Motors (accessed February 17, 2015).

Wilson, Mark. *The Electronic Encyclopedia of Chicago.* 2005. http://www. encyclopedia.chicagohistory.org/pages/2547.html (accessed February 17, 2015).

Wired. You Tube. July 16, 2013. https://www.youtube.com/ watch?v=8_lfxPI5ObM (accessed February 20, 2015).

Yarrow, Jay. businessinsider.com. October 15, 2010. http://www. businessinsider.com/apple-john-sculley-2010-10 (accessed February 20, 2015).